Essential Maths

1

Jayashri Bhattacharya

Preface

Mathematics has always been an integral part of human life. From times immemorial, Mathematics has been in our everyday life in various ways irrespective of our knowledge of the mathematical concepts involved in various activities. The school curriculum focuses on the mathematical concepts to cultivate thinking and developing the reasoning skills. It enables the students to take up a systematic approach to solve their daily life problems, aims at exploring multiple aspects of the subject and thus develop a passion for it.

Essential Maths is a series that strives to focus on the maximum involvement of children following an interactive learning pattern. It has been authored by a senior teacher who has been dedicating her years to the teaching of this subject. Following this series will help students to keep away from rote learning and develop their confidence. Their increased confidence and flexibility with numbers will help them handle abstractions and develop logical approach towards the subject. The review exercises help the learners assess their understanding of the concepts. This series also develops the potential of the learners for continuous and comprehensive evaluation, by inculcating the scholastics and co-scholastic skills. Its activity based interactive style will sharpen the learners' minds and make learning enriching and joyous. The books are beautifully illustrated which adds to the overall appeal of the series.

From the Author

Mathematics has always been an integral part of human life. We use mathematics in our everyday life in various ways without being aware of our knowledge of the mathematical concepts involved in the activity. School curriculum includes the study of Mathematics in order to focus on mathematical concepts which help to cultivate the thinking and reasoning skills. It is a systematic approach to enable students to solve their daily life problems. It also aims to allow the students to explore the multiple aspects of the subject and develop a passion for it.

The lab activities and exercises can be used by the teachers as a demonstrative tool in the Maths Lab.

Objectives of teaching Mathematics are:

- To develop an ability to think and reason mathematically
- To handle abstractions
- To cultivate a positive attitude towards mathematics following an interactive learning pattern to help the teacher ensure maximum involvement of the learners
- To increase confidence and flexibility of the learners when numbers are concerned
- To discourage rote learning
- To develop logical sense along with a passion for the subject

The series **Essential Maths** is a carefully graded series prepared in accordance with the new syllabus prescribed by the NCERT on the basis of CCE (Continuous and Comprehensive Evaluation). A remarkable feature of this series is that all the exercises are formed in such a manner that they begin with easy exercises and gradually progresses to difficult ones. The books are activity based and extensive drilling with integrated revision exercises form its key feature. All the books are full of colourful illustrations which make learning a joy! They also inculcate scholastic and co-scholastic skills in the learner.

I take this opportunity to thank a few people who have helped me write this series. They are Ms Seema Chawla my editor for continuously guiding me, my friend Ms Tapasi (Managing Editor, B Jain), my parents-in-law for encouraging me and Aurobindo, my husband, for being very supportive. Heartfelt thanks to Sofia and Shantanu, my kids. Without their suggestions and criticism, I would not have been able to undertake and complete this project.

Jayashri Bhattacharya

Contents

Pre-Number Concepts

1

Comparison

Big and small

Bird is small

Elephant is big

1. Tick (✓) the object which is big.

For comparison we say bigger or smaller.

Bigger

Smaller

2. Tick (✓) the bigger object, cross (×) the smaller object.

Tall and short

Write T for tall and S for short

When we compare we say taller and shorter.

1. Tick (✓) the taller.

2. Tick (✓) the shorter.

Near and far

The tree is near the house

The pond is far from the house.

1. Look at the picture and tick (✓) the object which is near the boy and cross (✗) the one which is far away.

2. Tick (✓) which is near the man and cross (✗) which is far.

On and under

The book is on the table.
The bag is under the table.

Top, middle and bottom

Top

Middle

Bottom

1. Draw a cherry on top of the cake.

2. Draw a pebble at the bottom of the bucket.

3. Tick (✓) which is at the bottom.

 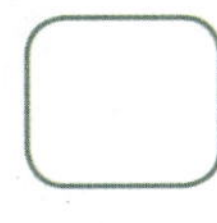

4. Tick (✓) which is at the top.

Above and below

1. Tick (✓) which is above.

More and less

More

Less

1. Colour the bunch that has more keys.

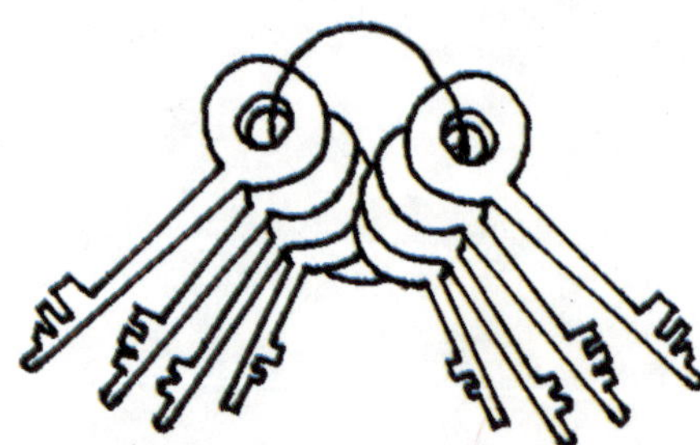

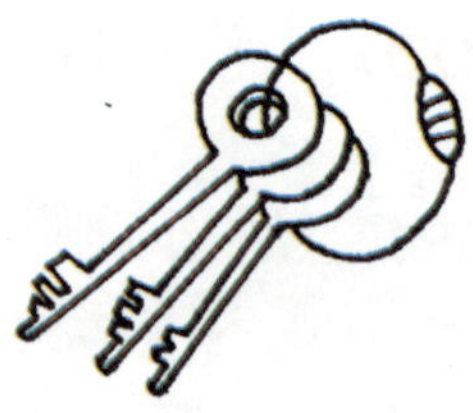

Longer and shorter

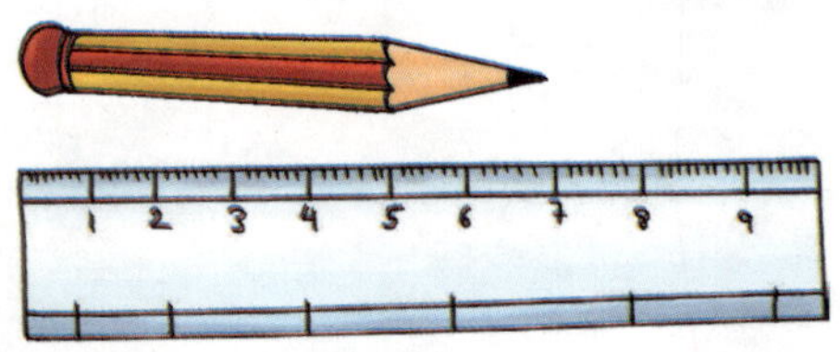

Ruler is longer

Rope is longer

Comparison

Tall Taller Tallest

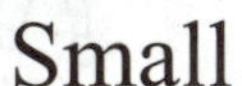

Small

Smaller

Smallest

Long

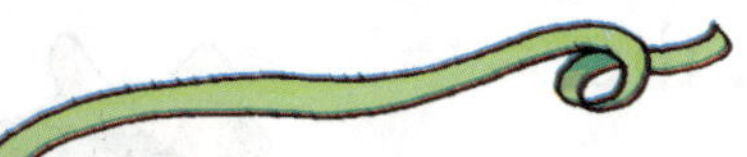

Longer

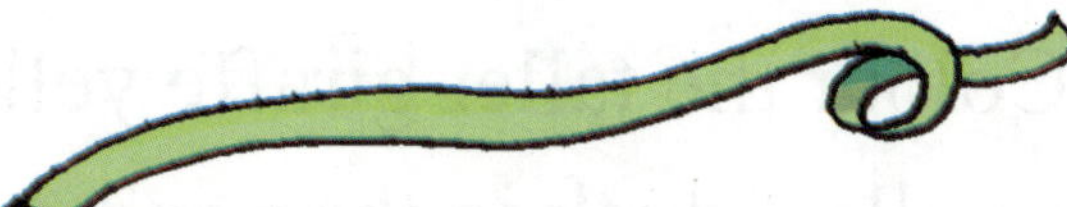

Longest

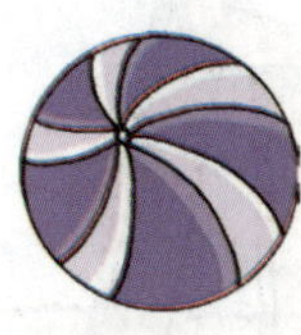

Big

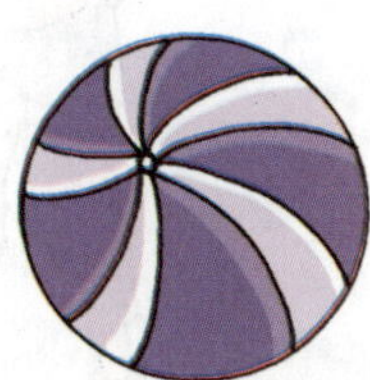

Bigger

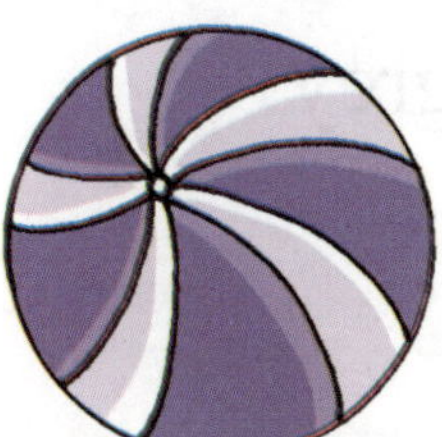

Biggest

Lab Activity

Colour the taller giraffe yellow, the smallest duck in the pond orange, the tree near the lake green, the horse under the tree brown, the biggest animal grey

Numbers (1-10)

2

Counting

Count the objects and learn to write the numbers.

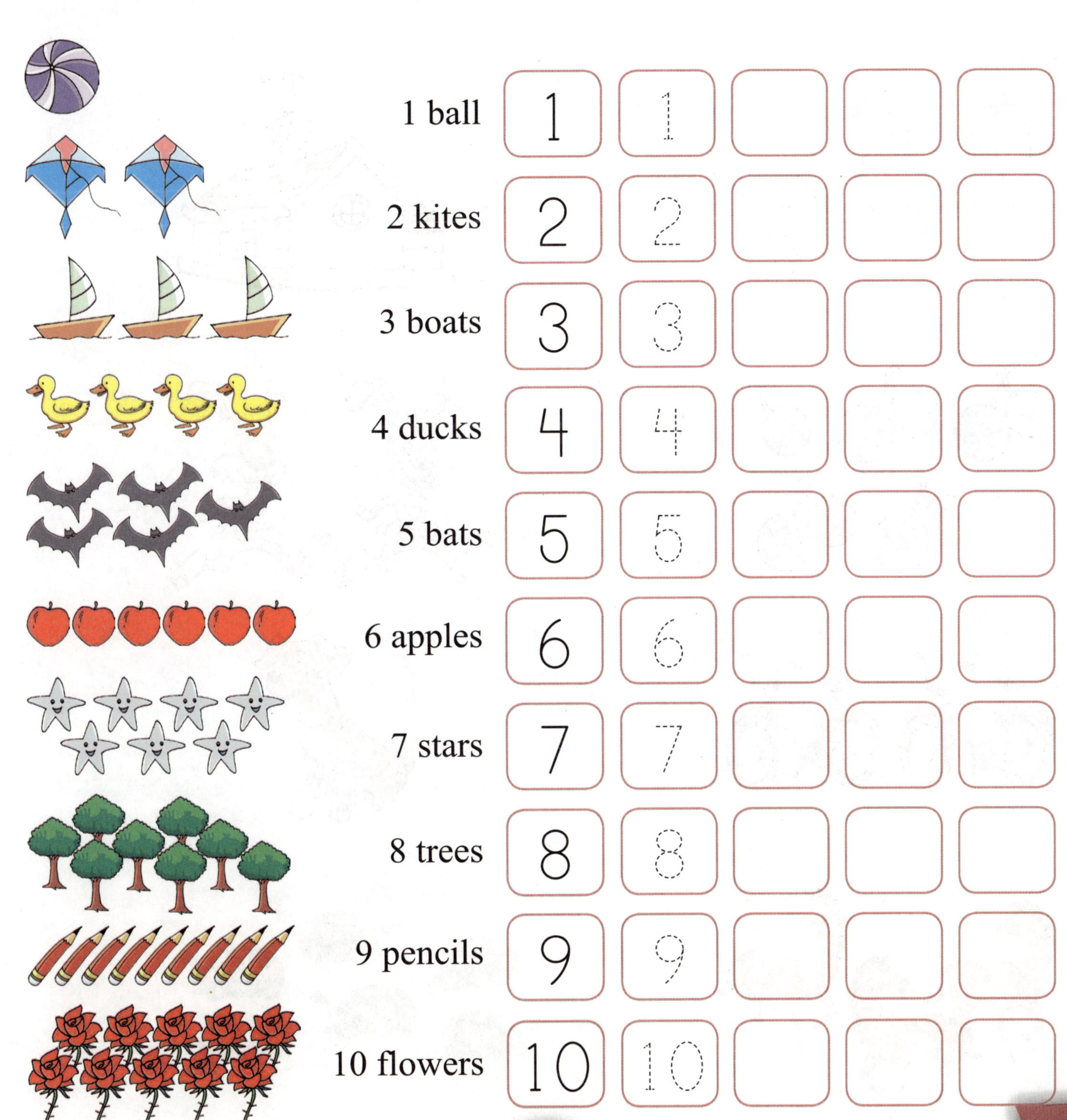

Count the objects and write how many are there.

Number Names

Count and write in the space provided.

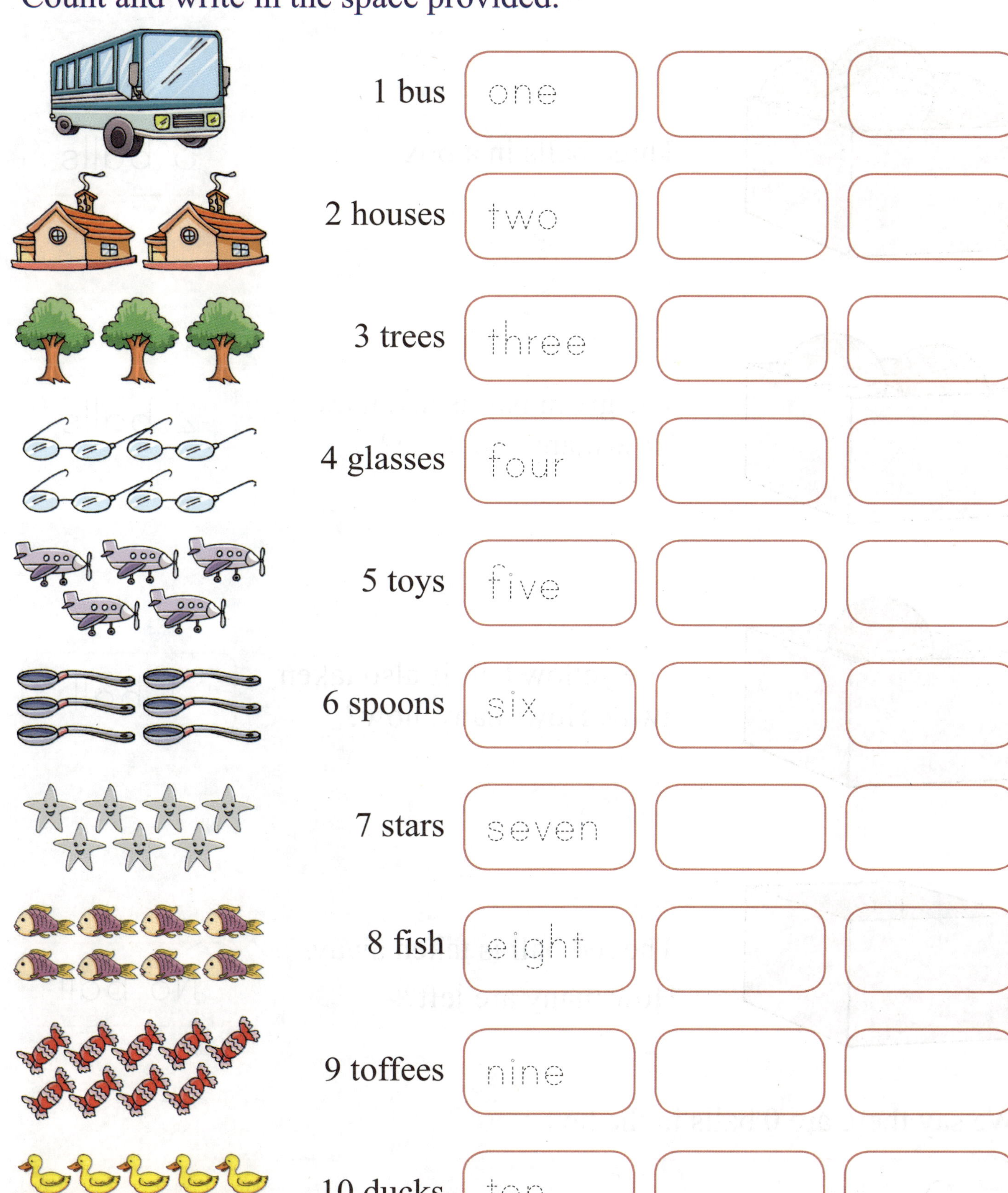

1 bus	one		
2 houses	two		
3 trees	three		
4 glasses	four		
5 toys	five		
6 spoons	six		
7 stars	seven		
8 fish	eight		
9 toffees	nine		
10 ducks	ten		

The Number '0'

Three balls in a box

3 balls

The green ball is taken away. How many are there?

2 balls

The yellow ball is also taken away. How many, now?

1 ball

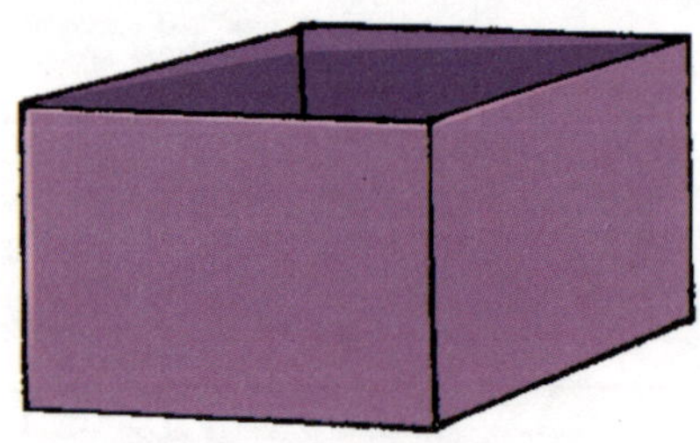

The red ball is taken away. How many are left?

No ball

We say there are 0 balls in the box.

Lab Activity

From the picture find out, write the numbers and its name.

How many boys? ______ ....

How many trees? ______ ....

How many marbles? ______ ....

Before, After and Between

0	1	2	3	4	5	6	7	8	9	10

Use the strip to write

What comes after

3			4	
5			9	
8			1	

What comes before

	3			1
	10			6
	7			8

What comes between

2		4		6		8		7		9
8		10		3		5		0		2
5		7		1		3		8		10

Greater than (>), Less than (<), Equal to (=)

Blue plate has ☐ toffees. Red plate has ☐ toffees.

Which plate has more toffees? Yes, the red plate .

6 is greater than 4. (6 > 4)

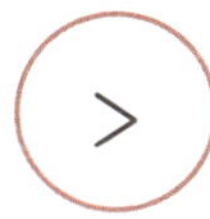

6 is greater than 4

7 is greater than 5. (7 > 5)

5 is less than 7

The pointed end of '>' is towards smaller number.

5 is less than 7

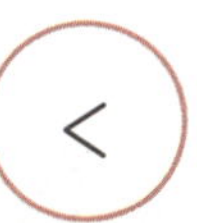

EXAMPLE

'EQUAL TO'

The plates have equal number of toffees.

Sign for equal to is '='

4 = 4

Fill in the boxes

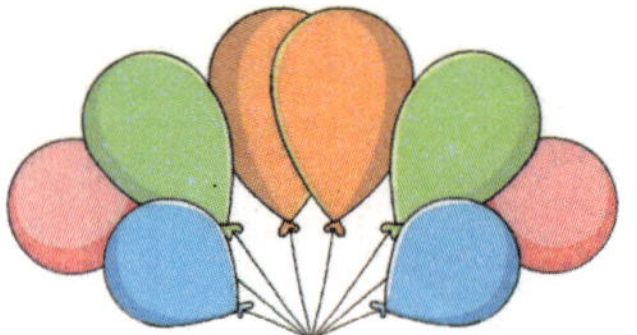
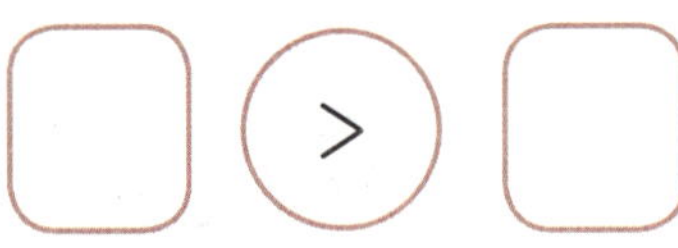

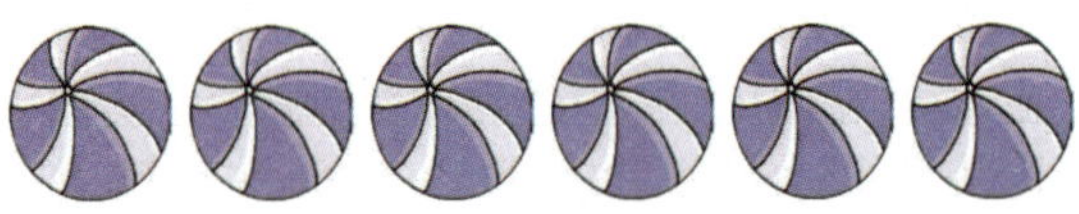

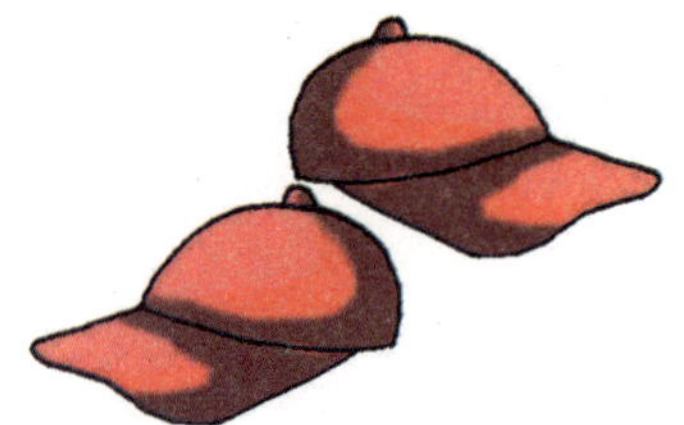

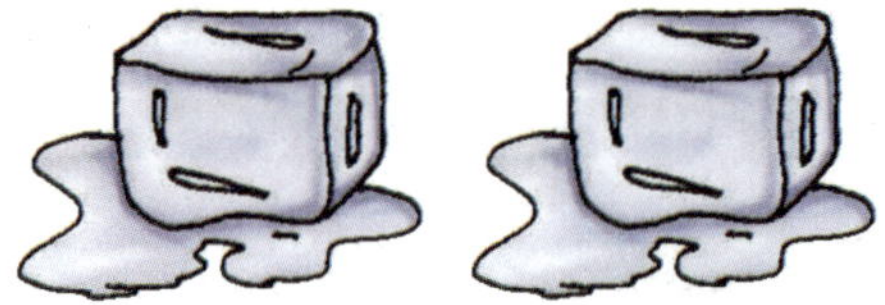

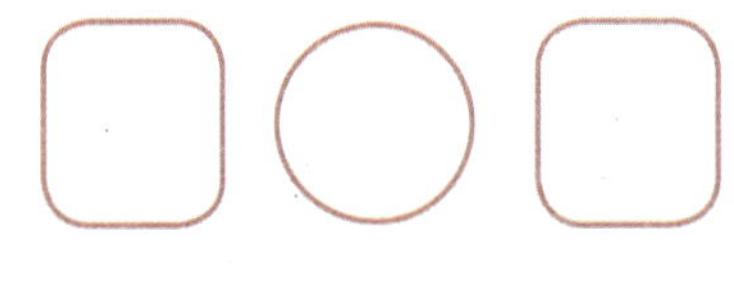

Fill in the correct signs (>, <, =).

3	<	4	2		3	5		0
8	=	8	2		10	4		6
9		4	1		8	10		7
5		6	3		3	0		1

Colour the smallest number blue.

7	9	10
6	1	5
10	4	0
2	5	9

Colour the greatest number green.

0	8 	6 
6	0 	1 
7	4 	10 
2	5 	9

Ascending Order

Ascending means moving from smallest to greatest. It is also known as increasing order.

Increasing order

EXAMPLE

Write the numbers from smallest to greatest.

9 1 6 5 → 1 5 6 9

Number 1 is the smallest. So it is written frist. This is the increasing order or ascending order.

Write the following numbers in the increasing order or ascending order

10 2 7 4 → 2 4 7 10

(These numbers are in the increasing order.)

Write the following in the increasing order. Write the smallest in black and the greatest in red.

				Answers			
6	9	3	1	1			9
4	8	2	10				
5	10	1	9				
3	6	5	4				

Descending Order

When numbers are written from greater to smallest it is said to be in the decreasing order or descending order.

Decreasing order

Write the numbers in decreasing order

4 3 1 9 ⟶ 9 4 3 1

Number 9 is the greatest. So it is written first. 1 is the smallest so it is written at the last.

7 2 6 3 ⟶ 7 6 3 2

Write the numbers in the decreasing order or descending order.

Write the greatest in pink and the smallest in green.

Answers

7	9	1	5				
9	2	6	4				
6	8	1	3				

REVIEW EXERCISE 1

Count and write

4 Four

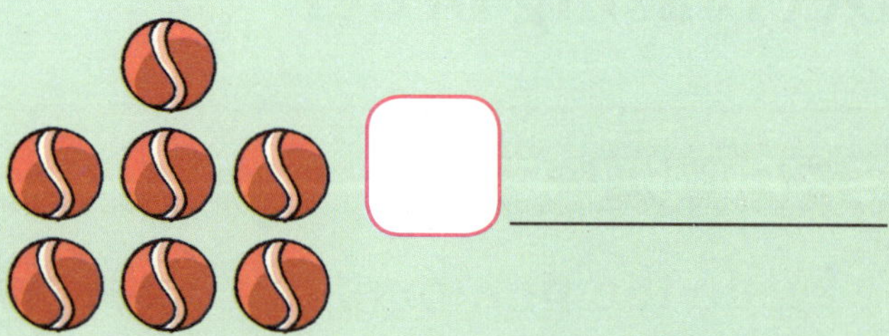

Colour the objects of the largest group.

1.

2.

Fill in the blanks with > and < or =

6  8

7  1

4  5

2  5

10  3

0  4

Fill in the boxes to complete the following rows.

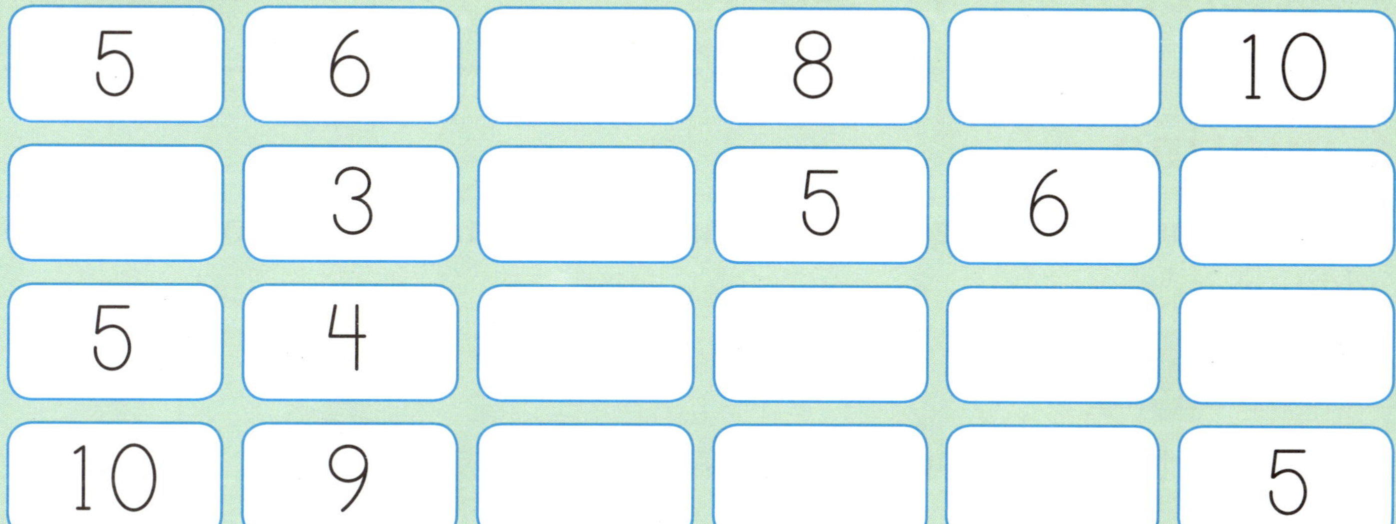

5	6		8		10
	3		5	6	
5	4				
10	9				5

Do as Directed

Colour 4 balloons red, 3 balloons green and 1 balloon pink.

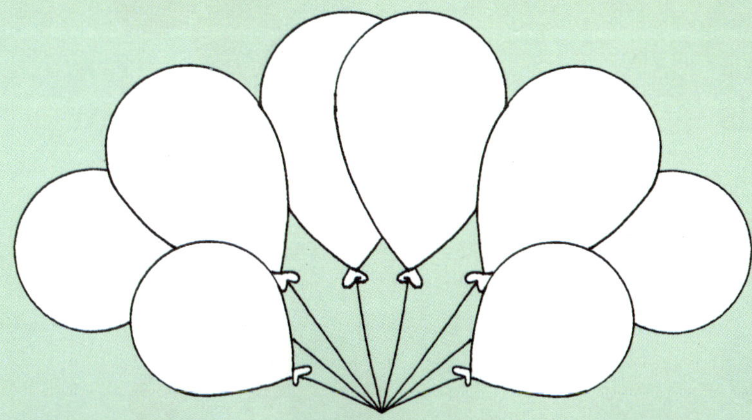

Circle the numbers greater than 4 in blue	3	5	1	6
Circle the numbers smaller than 8 in green	9	8	10	3
Circle the numbers greater than 6 in blue	7	8	6	1
Circle the numbers smaller than 3 in green	0	1	3	2

Addition (1-10)

Counting

When we put things together, we call it addition. The sign for addition is '+'.

EXAMPLE

4 + 4 = 8 Horizontal addition.

$$\begin{array}{r} 4 \\ +\ 4 \\ \hline 8 \\ \hline \end{array}$$

Vertical addition

In both cases answer is the same! It is said that the sum of 4 and 4 is 8.

	+		=	
2 beads	and	3 beads	=	5 beads
2	+	 3	=	5
	+		=	
6 balloons	and	2 balloons	=	8 balloons
6	+	2	=	8
	+		=	
4 books	and	3 books	=	7 books
4	+	3	=	7

Now add these

  +   = 

5 dolls and 1 doll = dolls

 +  = 

  +  = 

2 ice creams and 7 ice creams = ice creams

 +  = 

 + = 

1 fish and 0 fish = fish

 + = 

 +  = 

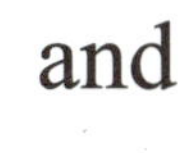  

6 caps and 4 caps = caps

 +  =

Addition on Number Line

This is a number line. Numbers 0, 1 to 10 are on it.

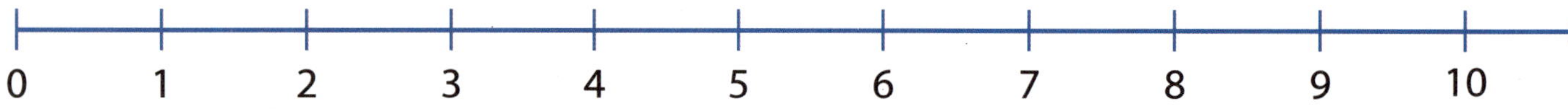

Let us add 2 and 3.

Go to 2

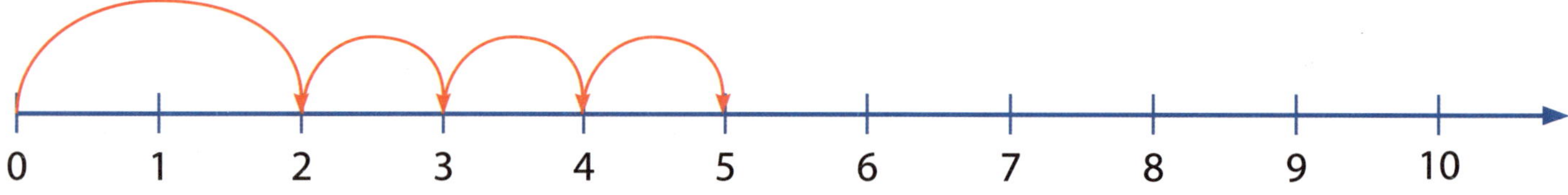

Then jump 3 steps. You reach 5.

2 + 3 = 5

Add these numbers using the number line.

a. Add 3 and 4

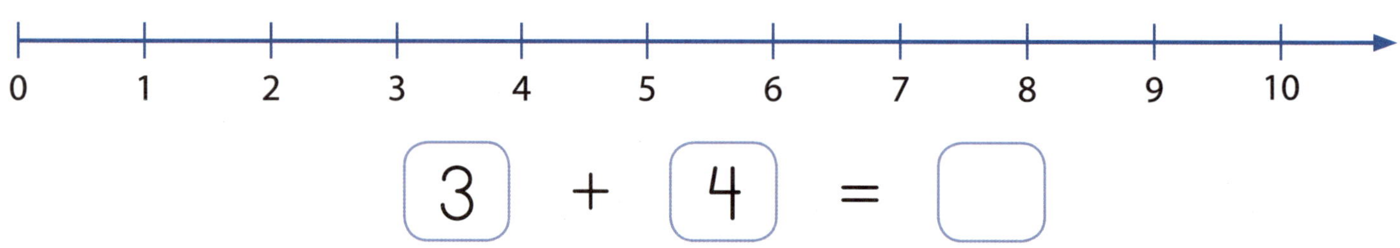

b. Add 1 and 7

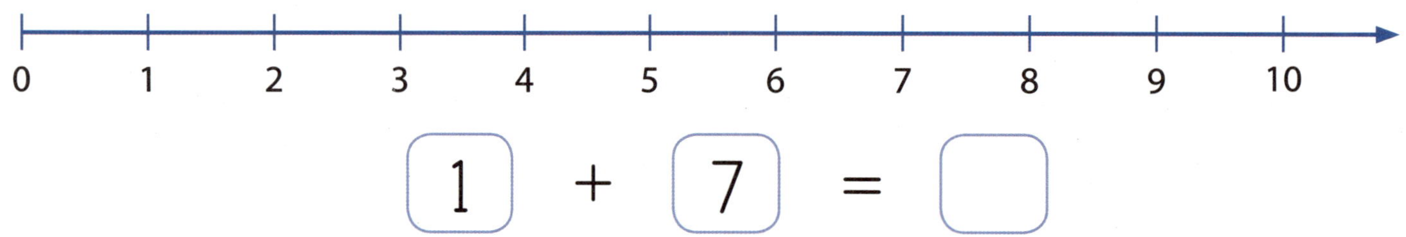

Vertical Additon

$$\begin{array}{r} 7 \\ +2 \\ \hline \\ \hline \end{array}$$

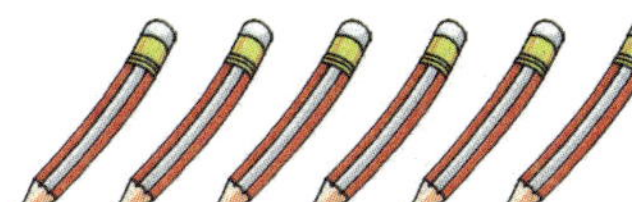

$$\begin{array}{r} 6 \\ +0 \\ \hline \\ \hline \end{array}$$

$$\begin{array}{r} 1 \\ +4 \\ \hline \\ \hline \end{array}$$

$$\begin{array}{r} 3 \\ +3 \\ \hline \\ \hline \end{array}$$

$$\begin{array}{r} 8 \\ +1 \\ \hline \\ \hline \end{array}$$

$$\begin{array}{r} 2 \\ +6 \\ \hline \\ \hline \end{array}$$

1. Add these

$$\begin{array}{r} 5 \\ +3 \\ \hline \\ \hline \end{array} \quad \begin{array}{r} 4 \\ +2 \\ \hline \\ \hline \end{array} \quad \begin{array}{r} 3 \\ +6 \\ \hline \\ \hline \end{array} \quad \begin{array}{r} 7 \\ +1 \\ \hline \\ \hline \end{array} \quad \begin{array}{r} 2 \\ +0 \\ \hline \\ \hline \end{array}$$

$$\begin{array}{r} 0 \\ +3 \\ \hline \\ \hline \end{array} \quad \begin{array}{r} 1 \\ +8 \\ \hline \\ \hline \end{array} \quad \begin{array}{r} 4 \\ +4 \\ \hline \\ \hline \end{array} \quad \begin{array}{r} 6 \\ +3 \\ \hline \\ \hline \end{array} \quad \begin{array}{r} 4 \\ +6 \\ \hline \\ \hline \end{array}$$

Add vertically

7 +3	8 +0	2 +5	6 +2	5 +0	5 +3
2 +7	3 +4	8 +1	5 +1	6 +1	4 +1
0 +7	9 +0	6 +3	1 +8	4 +2	3 +2

Add horizontally

3 + 3 = ☐

4 + 5 = ☐

1 + 0 = ☐

1 + 2 = ☐

7 + 0 = ☐

8 + 1 = ☐

1 + 2 = ☐

3 + 4 = ☐

9 + 1 = ☐

1 + 7 = ☐

Word Problems

Addition story sums

5 apples

4 oranges

3 Children

5 more children join

2 ducks

4 more ducks

6 crayons

3 more crayons

Subtraction (1-10)

Subtraction means 'taking away'; the sign for subtraction is '–'.

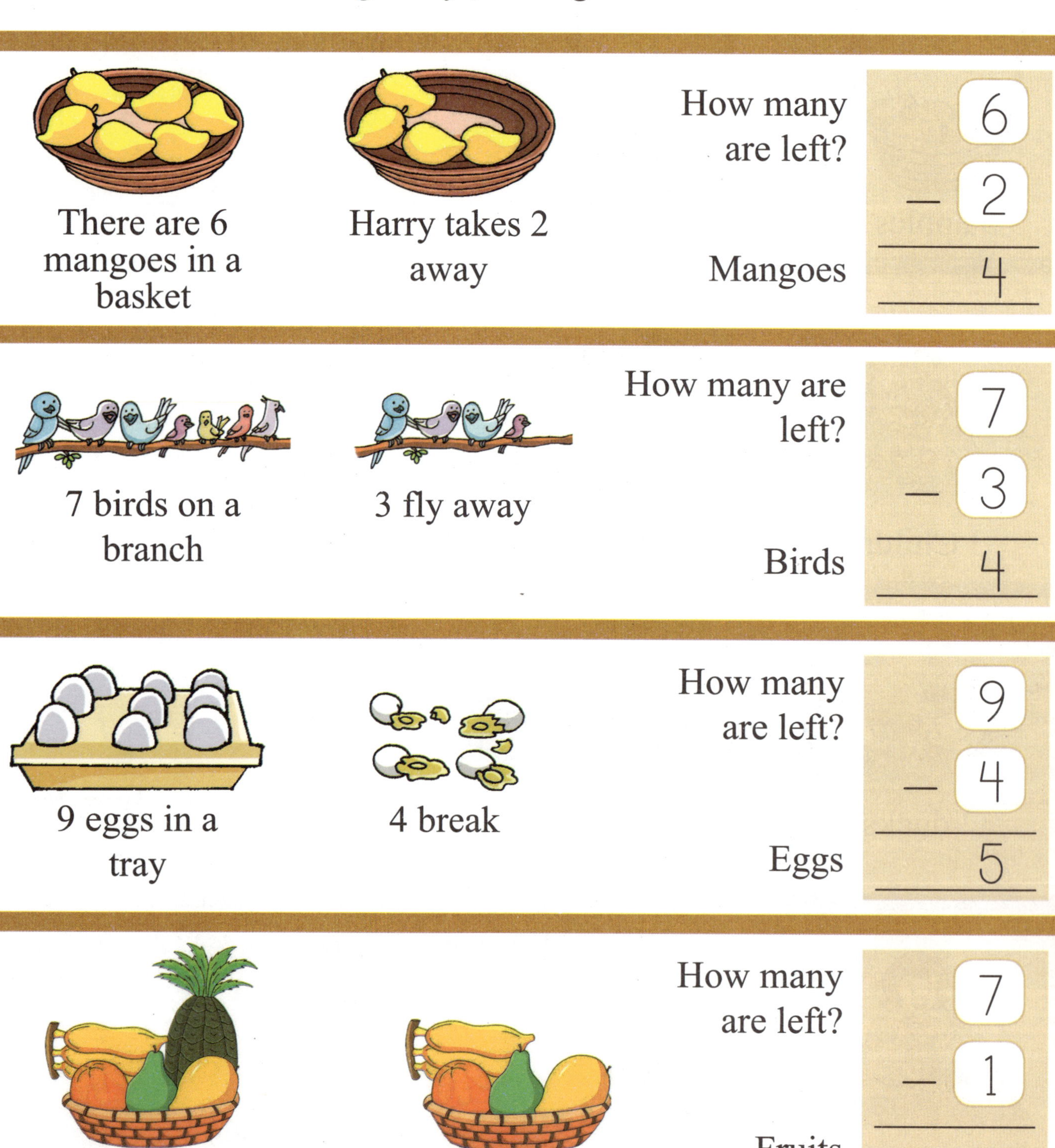

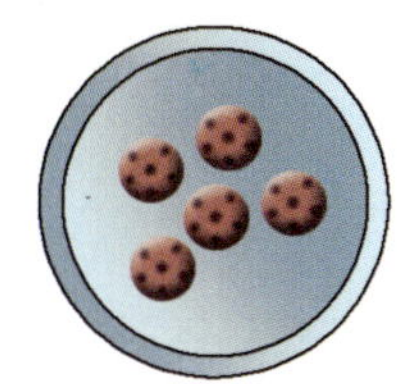 Take away 2 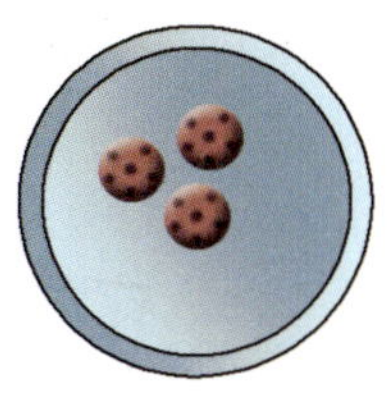

From 5 **take away** 2 3 left

5 — 2 = 3

From 6 sweets **take away** 1 = 5 **left**

6 — 1 = 5

Put a 'X' on the things you take away. Write what is left behind.

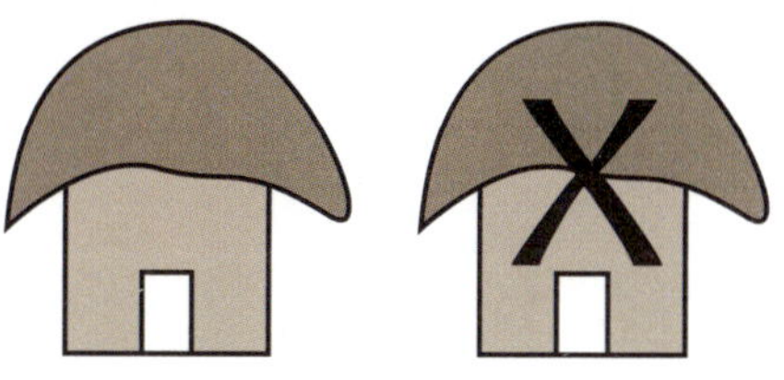

2 — 1 = 1

6 — 2 =

5 — 3 =

9 — 3 =

8 — 4 =

5 — 2 =

$10 - 6 = \square$

$5 - 5 = \square$

$6 - 1 = \square$

$7 - 5 = \square$

$7 - 4 = \square$

$4 - 0 = \square$

$5 - 4 = \square$

$8 - 8 = \square$

Vertical Subtraction

We write the greater number above and the smaller number below.

$$\begin{array}{r} 7 \\ -5 \\ \hline 2 \\ \hline \end{array}$$

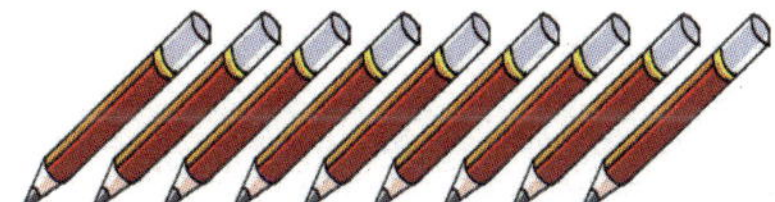

$$\begin{array}{r} 9 \\ -3 \\ \hline \\ \hline \end{array}$$

$$\begin{array}{r} 10 \\ -8 \\ \hline \\ \hline \end{array}$$

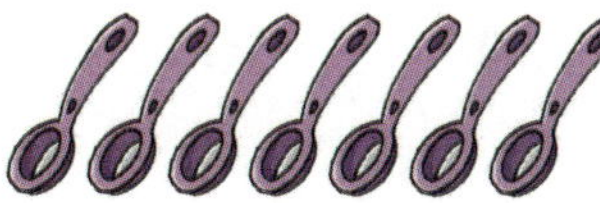

$$\begin{array}{r} 7 \\ -7 \\ \hline \\ \hline \end{array}$$

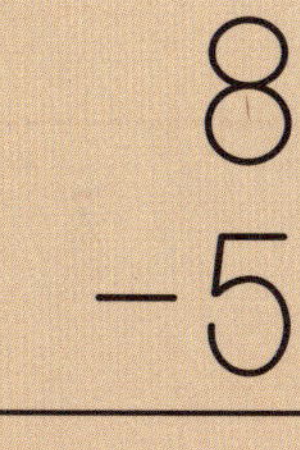

$$\begin{array}{r} 8 \\ -5 \\ \hline \\ \hline \end{array}$$

$$\begin{array}{r} 8 \\ -8 \\ \hline \\ \hline \end{array}$$

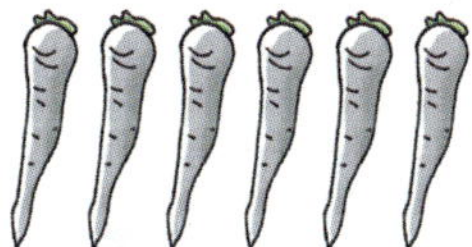

$$\begin{array}{r} 6 \\ -5 \\ \hline \\ \hline \end{array}$$

$$\begin{array}{r} 9 \\ -8 \\ \hline \\ \hline \end{array}$$

$$\begin{array}{r} 9 \\ -1 \\ \hline \\ \hline \end{array}$$

$$\begin{array}{r} 10 \\ -6 \\ \hline \\ \hline \end{array}$$

Subtraction on Number Line

Subtract 6 – 4

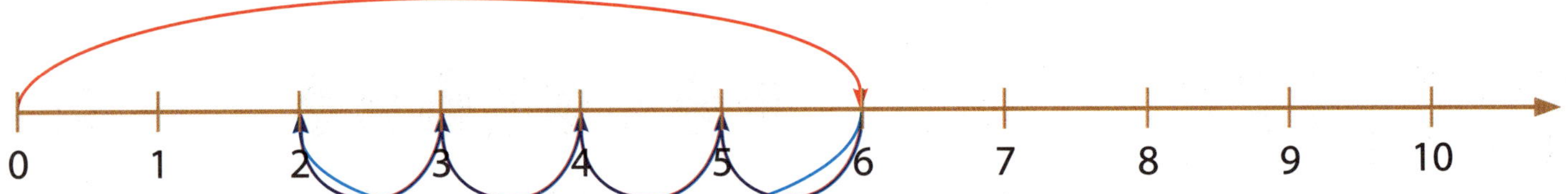

We start backwards from 6. Take 4 jumps and reach 2.

6 – 4 = 2

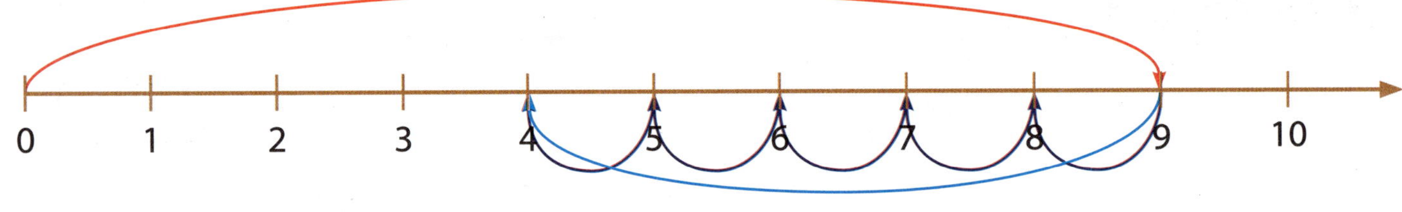

Use a number line to subtract and then fill in the boxes

a.

10 – 6 = ☐

b.

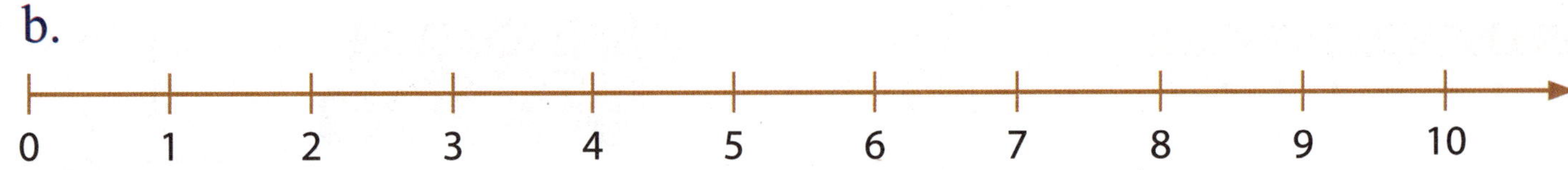

5 – 1 = ☐

c.

5 – 1 = ☐

d.

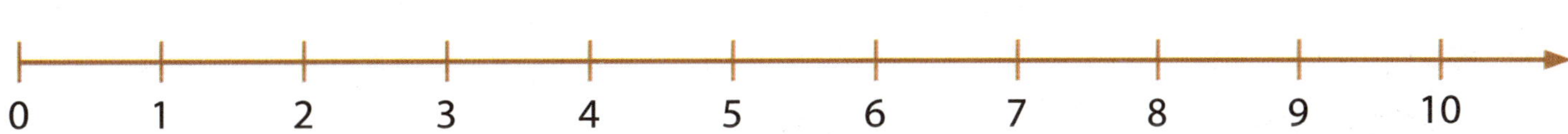

9 – 3 = ☐

Practice subtraction by solving the following

3 – 0 = ☐

3 – 1 = ☐

4 – 0 = ☐

4 – 1 = ☐

4 – 2 = ☐

6 – 4 = ☐

6 – 5 = ☐

7 – 1 = ☐

7 – 3 = ☐

7 – 5 = ☐

8 – 6 = ☐

9 – 0 = ☐

9 – 5 = ☐

10 – 5 = ☐

10 – 7 = ☐

Word Problems

Count and subtract

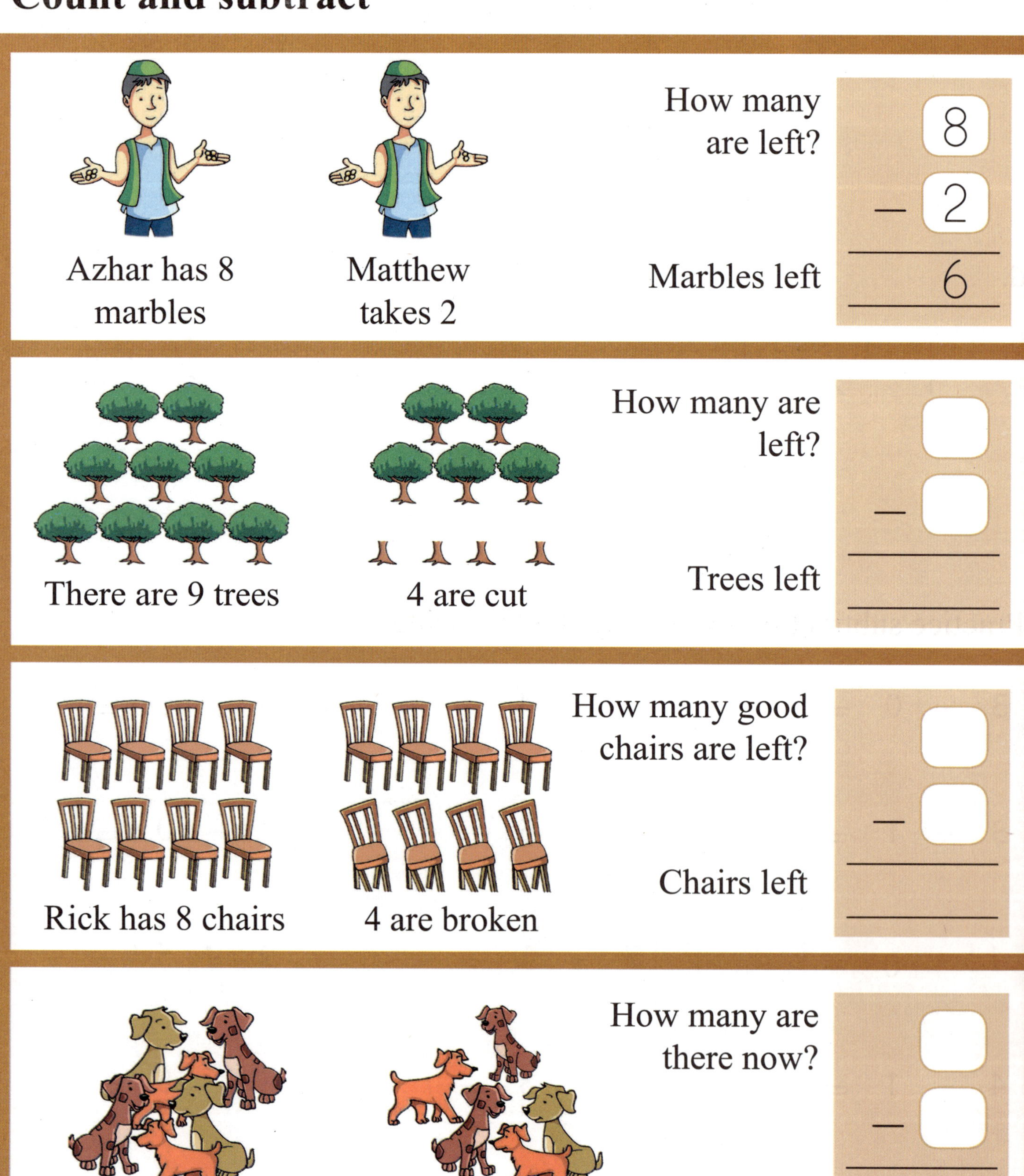

Mental Arithmetic

Fill in the grid.

Addition grid

+	2	5
4	6	9
3	5	8

+	2	0
6		
8		

+	1	2	3
4			
5			
6			

Subtraction grid

–	3	2
7	4	5
10		

–	4	0
5		
6		

–	0	7	8
8			
9			
10			

Fill in to find.

+	1	2	3	4	5	6	7	8	9	10
0										
1				5						
2	3									
3						9				
4			7							
5										
6										
7										
8		10								
9										

Lab Activity

Teacher can give different objects like ice cream sticks, pencils, marbles, beads etc and ask children to put them in groups of 10 each.

These will be used in the next chapters.

2-Digit Numbers (11-20)

5

Lab Activity

10 ice cream sticks are put together to make a bundle of 10.

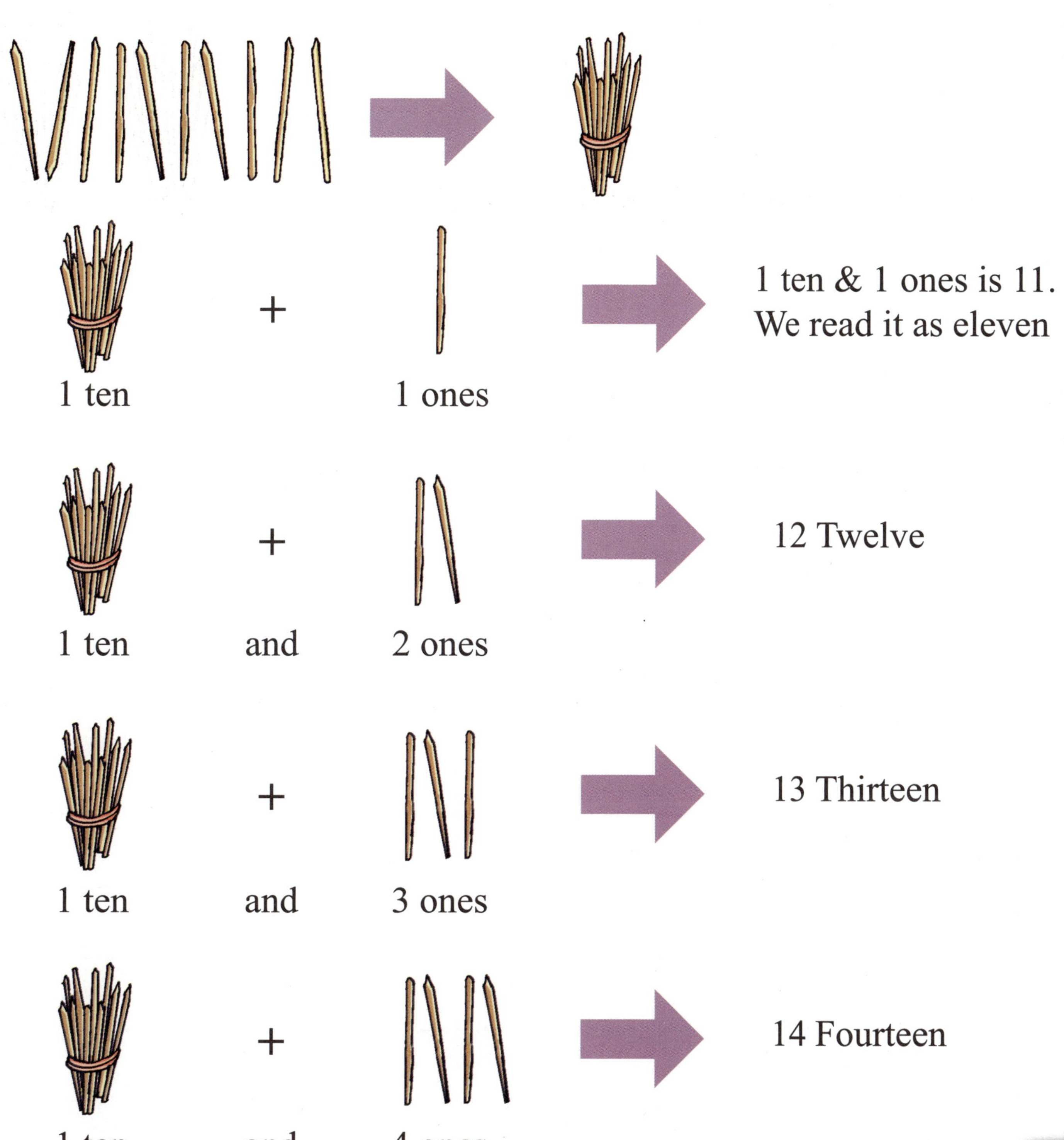

Now fill in the boxes

1 ten + 5 ones = fifteen

☐ ten + ☐ ones = sixteen

☐ ten + ☐ ones = seventeen

☐ ten + ☐ ones = eighteen

☐ ten + ☐ ones = nineteen

We can make 1 more bundle of the 10 sticks.

1 ten + 1 ten = 2 tens = 20 twenty

Write counting from 11 to 20 also learn to write the number names.

Write 11-20

11	11						eleven
12	12						twelve
13	13						
14	14						
15	15						
16	16						
17	17						
18	18						
19	19						
20	20						twenty

Writing Number Names

10	+	1	=	11	eleven	....	....	....
10	+	2	=	12	twelve	....	....	....
10	+		=	13	thirteen	....	....	....
	+		=	14	fourteen	....	....	....
	+		=	15	fifteen	....	....	....
	+		=	16	sixteen	....	....	....
	+		=	17	seventeen	....	....	....
	+		=	18	eighteen	....	....	....
	+		=	19	nineteen	....	....	....
	+		=	20	twenty	....	....	....

Comparison of Numbers (1-20)

Greater than (>) and less than (<)

Use this number line and fill '>' or '<' in the ◯ given below.

20 ◯ 16	11 ◯ 19	14 ◯ 17
18 ◯ 10	12 ◯ 14	16 ◯ 13
13 ◯ 20	15 ◯ 20	19 ◯ 14
17 ◯ 16	9 ◯ 11	15 ◯ 10
8 ◯ 18	13 ◯ 16	18 ◯ 8
20 ◯ 19	0 ◯ 15	15 ◯ 19
11 ◯ 09	14 ◯ 20	20 ◯ 13

Before				After			
	20		14	18		12	
	17		15	15		14	
	11		19	16		19	
	13		9	11		13	

Fill in the boxes with what comes 'between'.

13		15	9		11	17		19
18		20	12		14	13		15
14		16	10		12	15		17
11		13	16		18	8		10
15		17	4		6	0		2
13		15	18		20	5		7
11		13	1		3	2		4

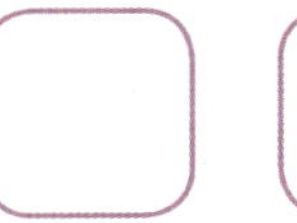

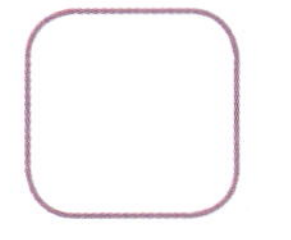

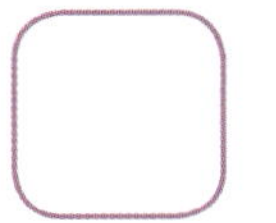

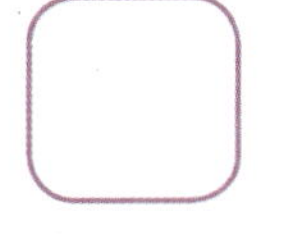

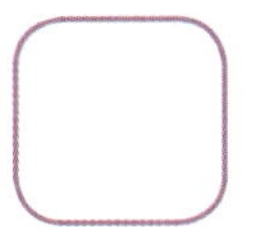
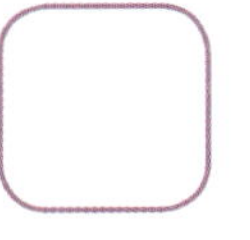
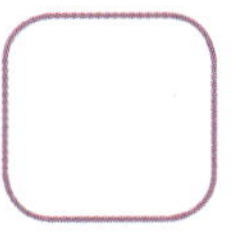
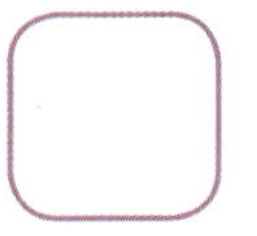
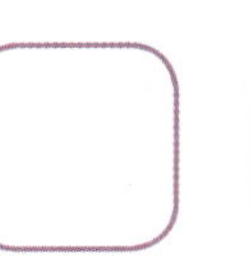

Addition (1-19)

6

Group in tens & ones and then add.

	+		=		and		=	13
7	+	6		1 ten	+	3 ones		
	+		=		and		=	16
9	+	7		1 ten	+	6 ones		
	+		=		and		=	20
10	+	10		1 ten	+	1 ten		
	+		=		and		=	
8	+	5		1 ten	+	3 ones		
	+		=		and		=	
5	+	9		ten	+	ones		
	+		=		and		=	
4	+	8		ten	+	ones		

Add by drawing dots.

11 + 4 → 15	
12 + 6 →	
9 + 8 →	
4 + 12 →	
14 + 6 →	
13 + 7 →	
17 + 1 →	
16 + 0 →	
4 + 15 →	

Lab Activity

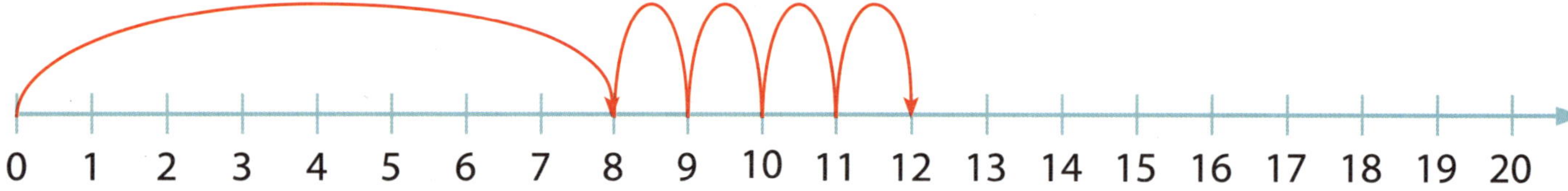

8 + 4 = 12

Teacher can draw the number line on the floor and ask students to perform the additions. Students need not draw; but can just perform the addition and write in the space provided.

6 +9 ____	15 +5 ____	12 +6 ____	8 +7 ____	10 +8 ____	7 +9 ____
7 +11 ____	12 +5 ____	3 +9 ____	13 +2 ____	14 +3 ____	9 +11 ____
11 +4 ____	7 +8 ____	16 +4 ____	17 +2 ____	15 +9 ____	17 +2 ____
10 +6 ____	8 +5 ____	18 +2 ____	11 +4 ____	9 +3 ____	15 +3 ____

Word Problems

Addition story sums

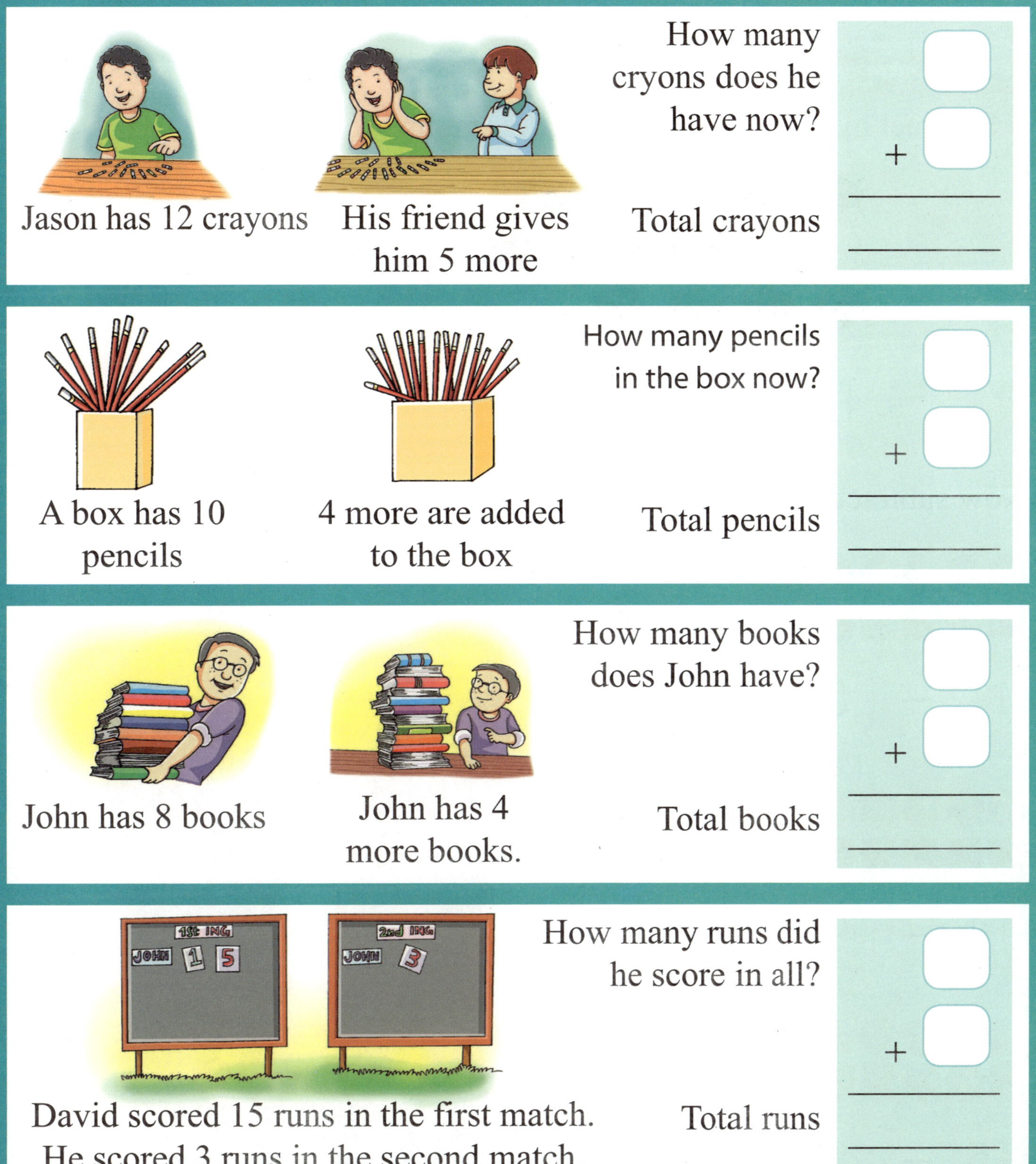

Subtraction (1-19)

7

EXAMPLE

Subtract by crossing out the smaller number of objects.

13 − 6 = 7

Now subtract by using marbles

11 − 5 = ☐

12 − 2 = ☐

14 − 9 = ☐

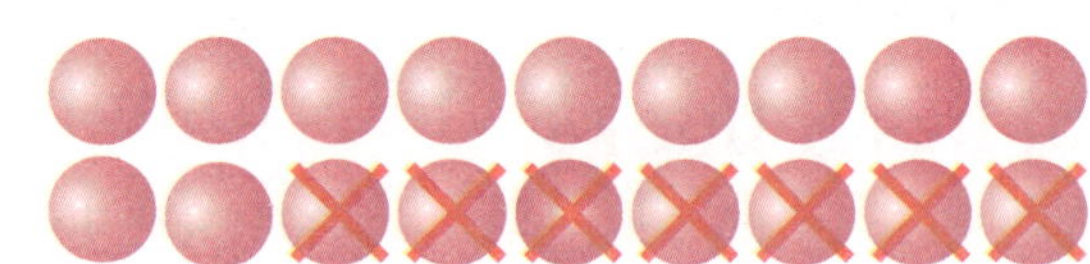

18 − 7 = ☐

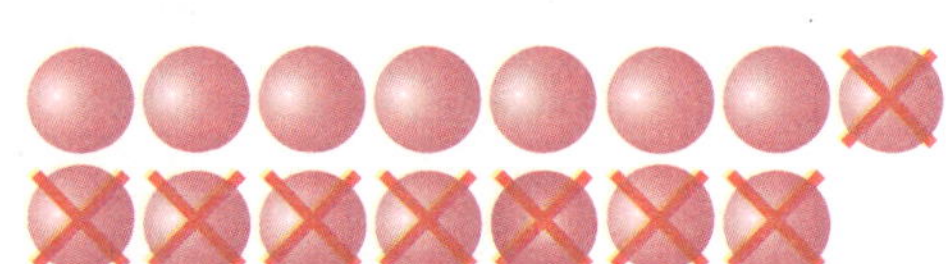

15 − 8 = ☐

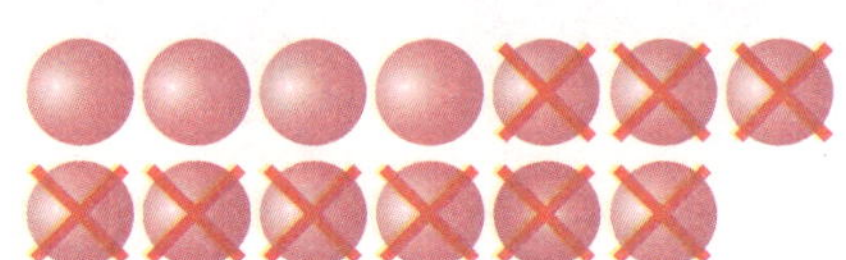

13 − 9 = ☐

Subtract

19
−7
____

16
−8
____

17
−9
____

12
−0
____

11
−8
____

15
−5
____

16
−9
____

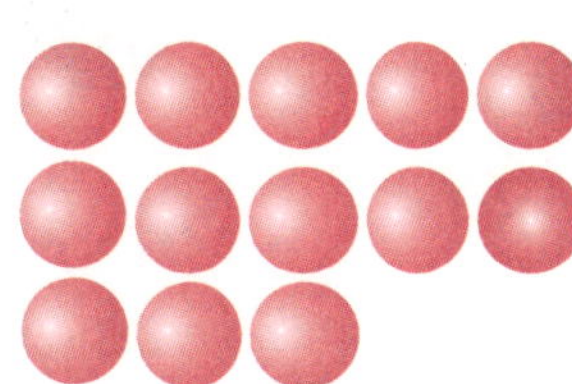

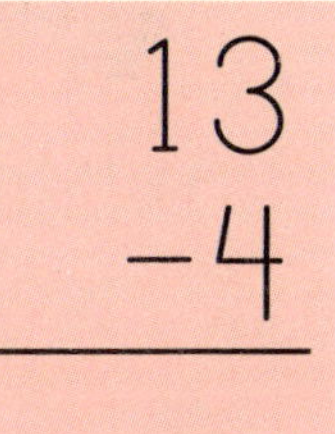

13
−4
____

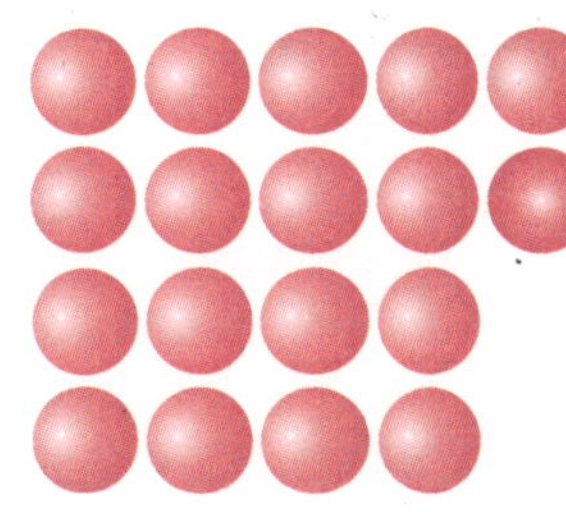

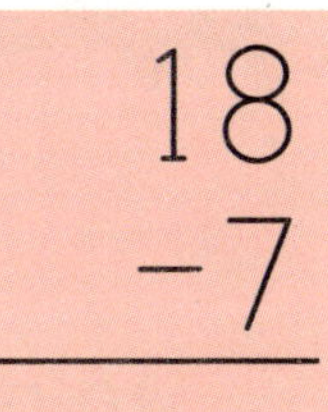

18
−7
____

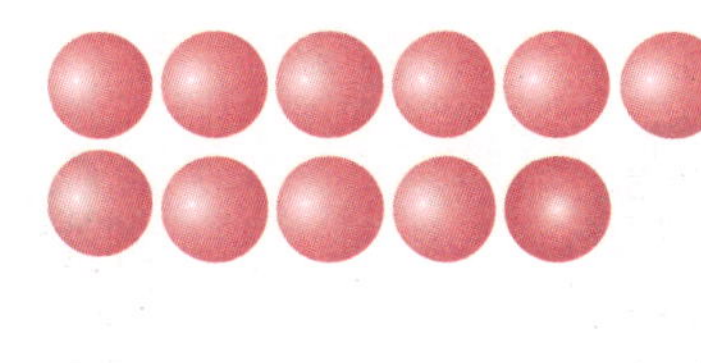

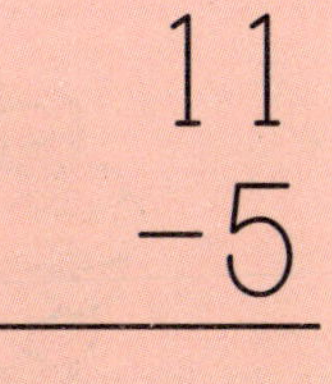

11
−5
____

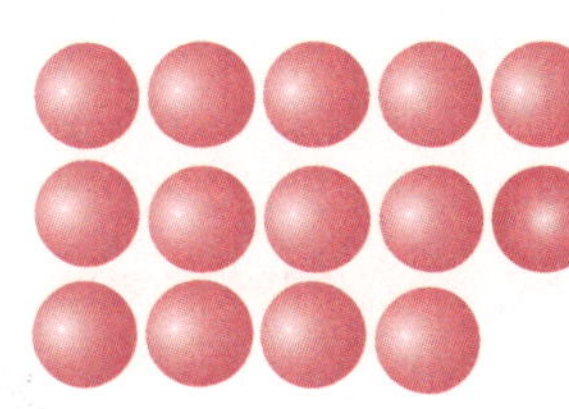

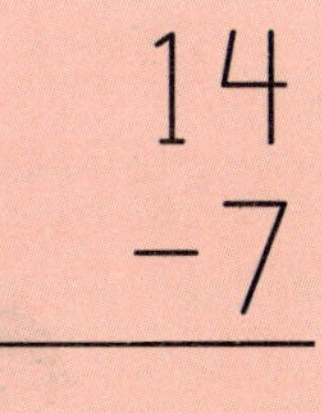

14
−7
____

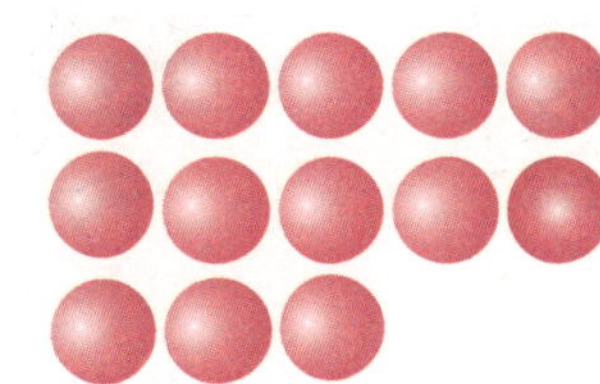

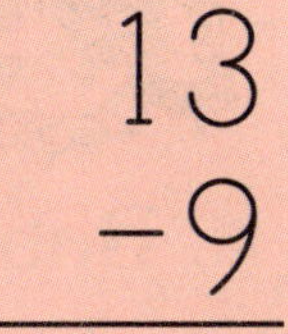

13
−9
____

Word Problems

Subtraction

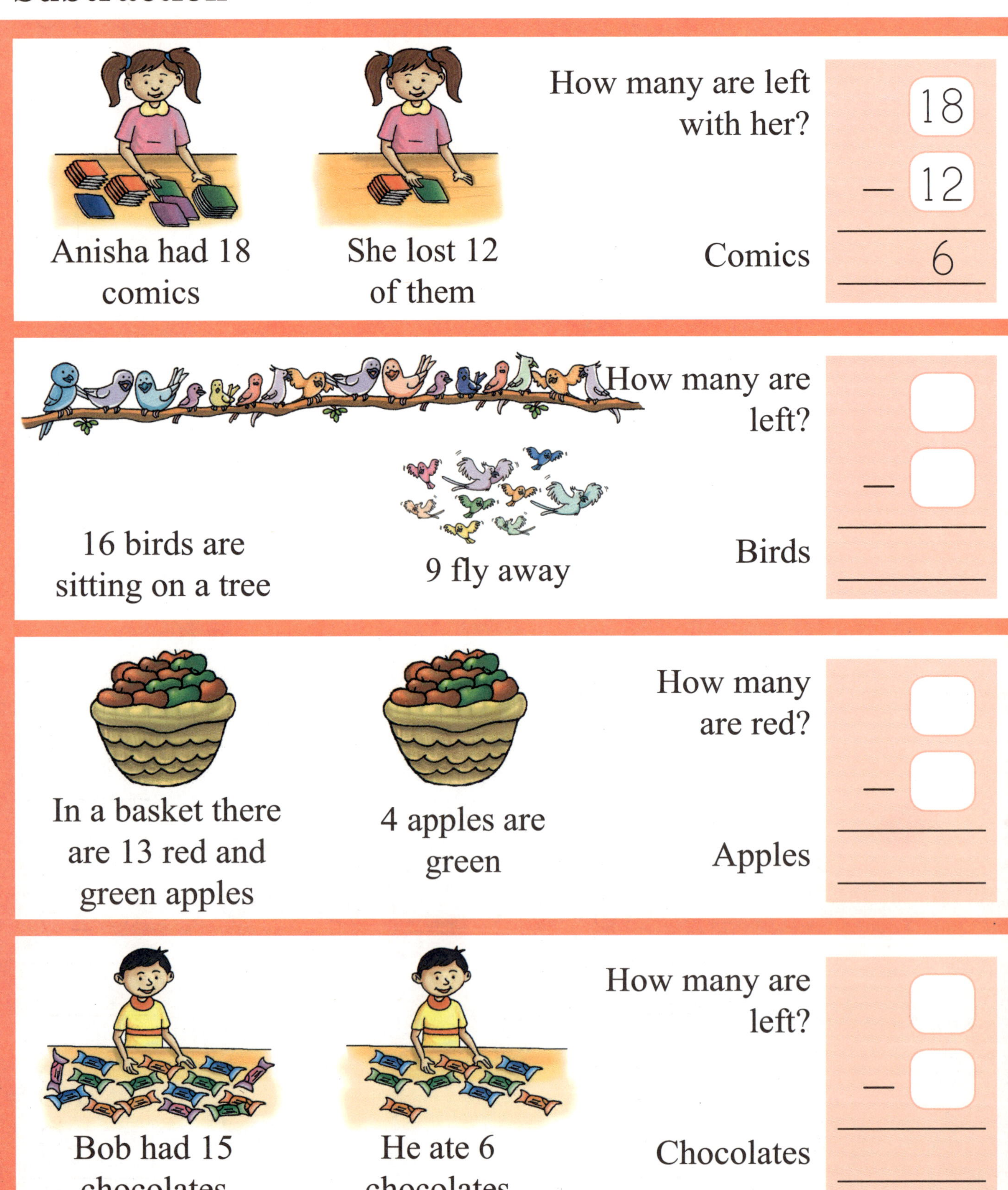

There are 19 chairs in a room

People are sitting on 16 of these chairs

How many are vacant?

People

Lewis has 13 toy cars

Kevin has 16 toy cars

How many more cars does Kevin have?

Toys

Karan is 7 years old

Sam is 14 years old

By how many years is Sam older?

Years

A class has 20 students

13 of them went on a picnic

How many students did not go?

Students

Place Value

8

You have already learnt 1-digit numbers from 1 to 9.
Now, let us move ahead....

 and  = 

7 + 1 = 8

 and  = 

9 + 1 = 10

Tens Ones

9

+ 0 =

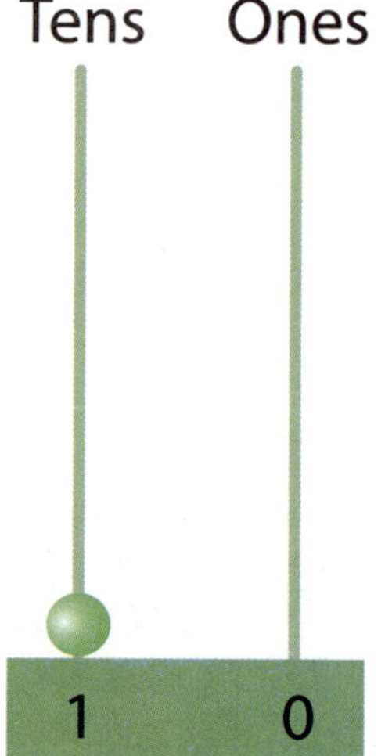

This is an **abacus**
A stick cannot have more than 9 beads

This is how we show 10 on **abacus**

1, 2, 3, 4, 5, 6, 7, 8 and 9 are single digit numbers. 10 is a **2-digit** number.

In the abacus there are separate sticks to show different places. For tens we move to the next stick on the left hand of ones stick.

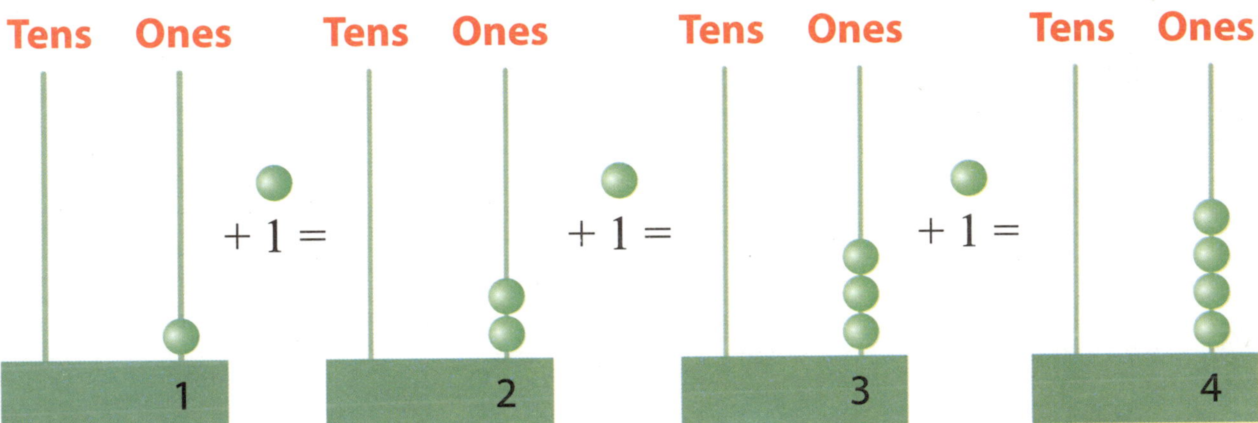

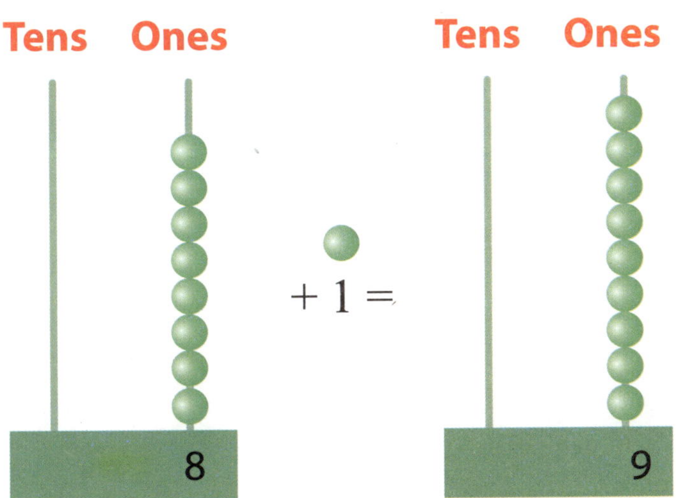

A stick can have only 9 beads.
If we put 1 more it is 10

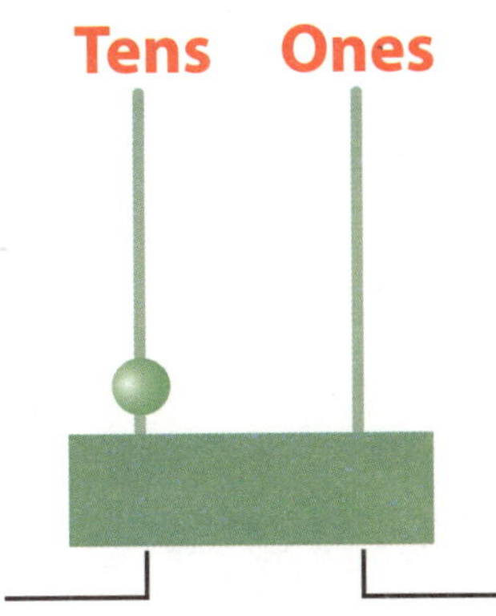

This is tens.

This is for single digits. It is 'ones'

So, if we have 15, it is

Tens Ones

1 5

Let us show 2-digit numbers on the abacus.

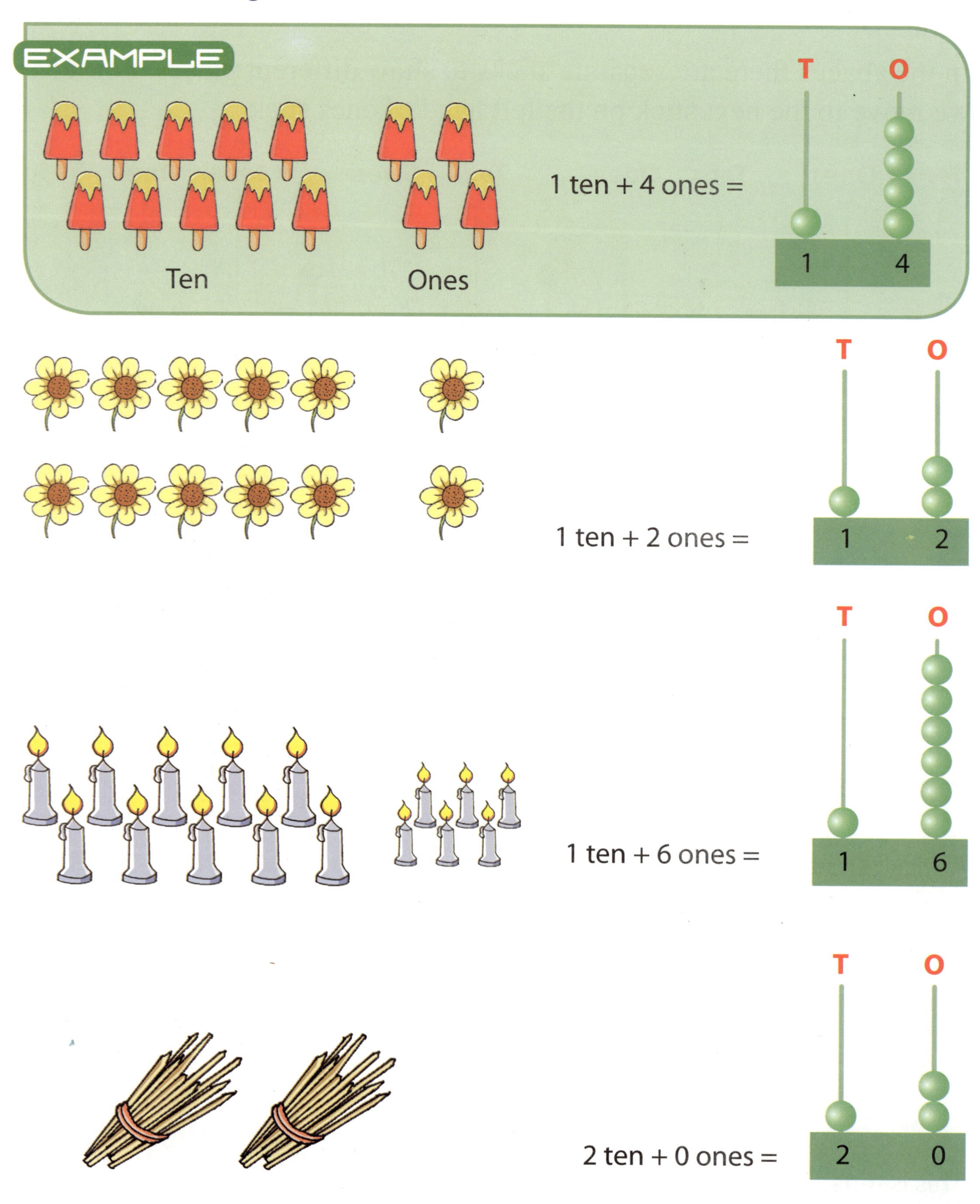

Ordinal Numbers

9

Ordinal numbers tells us about the order or positions of things. These animals are in a queue.

Tick (✓) who is first?

☐ Lion ☐ Zebra ☐ Rabbit

Tick (✓) who is last?

☐ Lion ☐ Monkey ☐ Peacock

Tick (✓) who is second?

☐ Giraffe ☐ Monkey ☐ Peacock

Order of months

January	First
February	Second
March	Third
April	Fourth
May	Fifth
June	Sixth
July	Seventh
August	Eighth
September	Ninth
October	Tenth
November	Eleventh
December	Twelfth

Number the boys according to their position in the race.

A	N	I	M	A	L	S
1	2	3	4	5	6	7

1. The first letter is A.
2. The second letter is ___.
3. The sixth letter is ___.
4. The ______ letter is L.
5. The ________ letter is M.

Days of the week

Monday	First
Tuesday	Second
Wednessday	Third
Thursday	Fourth
Friday	Fifth
Saturday	Sixth
Sunday	Seventh

REVIEW EXERCISE 2

Fill in the boxes

1	ten	+	4	ones	=	14
2	tens	+		ones	=	
1	ten	+		ones	=	10
3	ten	+		ones	=	30

1	ten	+	9	ones	=	
	ten	+		ones	=	16
	ten	+		ones	=	17
	ten	+		ones	=	18

Fill in the boxes

4	+	16	=	
6	+		=	11
15	–	12	=	
14	–	6	=	

3	+	13	=	
8	+	6	=	
11	–	3	=	
12	–		=	0

4	+	10	=	
9	+		=	18
17	–	5	=	
6	+	11	=	

T O	T O	T O	T O
14	15	19	20
+5	−7	−11	−13
___	___	___	___

T O	T O	T O	T O
13	10	17	14
+6	+9	−8	−9
___	___	___	___

First	______	______	______	______	______	______	Eighth

Follow these instructions and colour the boxes given above

1. Colour the third square green.
2. Colour the fifth square purple.
3. Colour the seventh square yellow.
4. Colour the square before third blue.
5. Colour the square after seventh orange.
6. Colour the square before blue red.
7. Colour the remaining pink.

FUN TIME

13 5 7 10 17

5 friends play cricket and they are in one team. Guess their T-shirt numbers.

Jacob says, 'My number is the same as the number of fingers on my two hands.' His number is ___________

Samuel says, 'My number is 3 less than Jacob's number'. His number is ___________

Aamir says, 'My number is the sum of the above two'. His number is ___________

Danny says, 'My number is the smallest?' His number is ___________

What is Zamir's number? ___________

Understanding Numbers (21-100)

10

Numbers 21-30

	2 tens	1 ones	=	21	Twenty-one
	2 tens	2 ones	=	22	Twenty-two
	2 tens	3 ones	=	23	Twenty-three
	2 tens	ones	=		Twenty-four
	2 tens	ones	=		Twenty-five
	2 tens	ones	=		Twenty-six
	2 tens	ones	=		Twenty-seven
	2 tens	ones	=		Twenty-eight
	2 tens	ones	=		Twenty-nine
	3 tens	ones	=		Thirty

Numbers 31-40

	3 tens	1 ones	=	31	Thirty-one
	3 tens	2 ones	=		Thirty-two
	tens	ones	=		Thirty-three
	tens	ones	=		Thirty-four
	tens	ones	=		Thirty-five
	tens	ones	=		Thirty-six
	tens	ones	=		Thirty-seven
	tens	ones	=		Thirty-eight
	tens	ones	=		Thirty-nine
	4 tens	0 ones	=		Forty

Numbers 41-50

	4 tens	1 ones	= 41	Forty-one
	4 tens	2 ones	=	Forty-two
	tens	ones	=	Forty-three
	tens	ones	=	Forty-four
	tens	ones	=	Forty-five
	tens	ones	=	Forty-six
	tens	ones	=	Forty-seven
	tens	ones	=	Forty-eight
	tens	ones	=	Forty-nine
	tens	ones	= 50	Fifty

Numbers 51-60

	5 tens	1 ones	= 51	Fifty-one
	5 tens	2 ones	= 52	Fifty-two
	tens	ones	= 53	Fifty-three
	tens	ones	= 54	Fifty-four
	tens	ones	= 55	Fifty-five
	tens	ones	= 56	Fifty-six
	tens	ones	= 57	Fifty-seven
	tens	ones	= 58	Fifty-eight
	tens	ones	= 59	Fifty-nine
	tens	ones	= 60	Sixty

Numbers 61-70

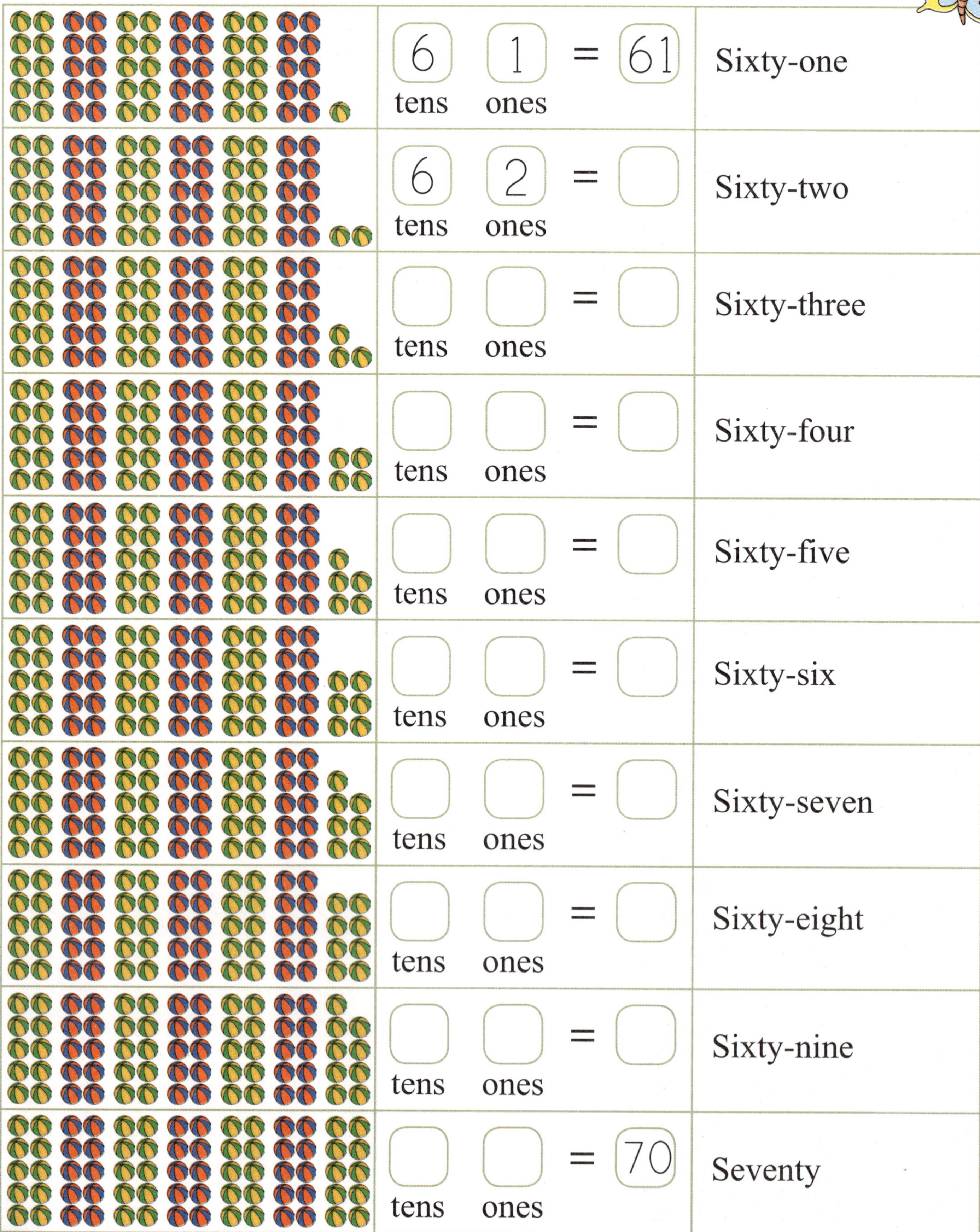

6 tens	1 ones	=	61	Sixty-one
6 tens	2 ones	=		Sixty-two
tens	ones	=		Sixty-three
tens	ones	=		Sixty-four
tens	ones	=		Sixty-five
tens	ones	=		Sixty-six
tens	ones	=		Sixty-seven
tens	ones	=		Sixty-eight
tens	ones	=		Sixty-nine
tens	ones	=	70	Seventy

Numbers 71-80

	7 tens 1 ones	= 71	Seventy-one
	7 tens 2 ones	= 72	Seventy-two
	tens ones	= 73	Seventy-three
	tens ones	= 74	Seventy-four
	tens ones	= 75	Seventy-five
	tens ones	= 76	Seventy-six
	tens ones	= 77	Seventy-seven
	tens ones	= 78	Seventy-eight
	tens ones	= 79	Seventy-nine
	tens ones	= 80	Eighty

Numbers 81-90

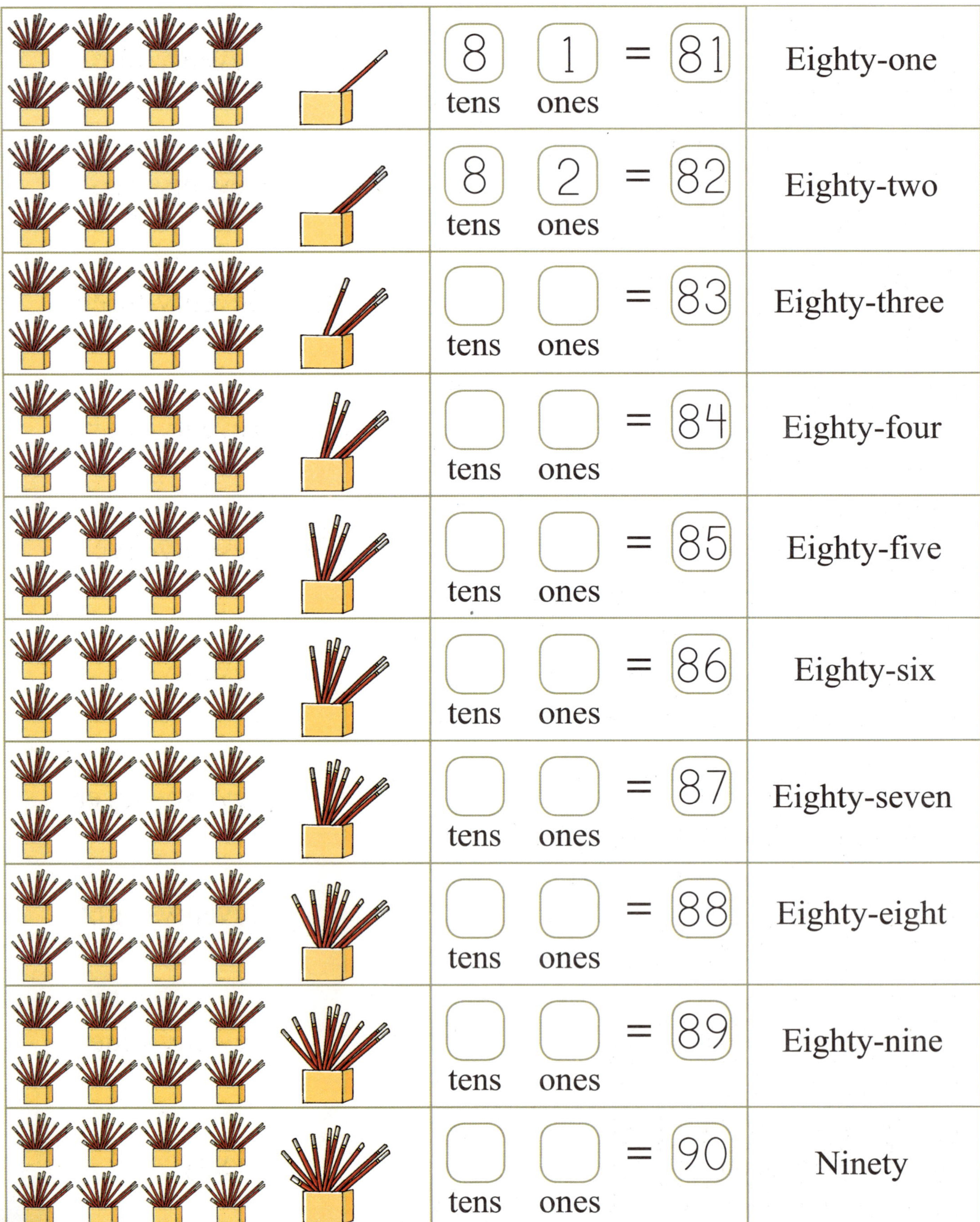

	tens	ones	=	Number	Name
	8	1	=	81	Eighty-one
	8	2	=	82	Eighty-two
			=	83	Eighty-three
			=	84	Eighty-four
			=	85	Eighty-five
			=	86	Eighty-six
			=	87	Eighty-seven
			=	88	Eighty-eight
			=	89	Eighty-nine
			=	90	Ninety

Numbers 91-100

	9 tens	1 ones	=	91	Ninety-one
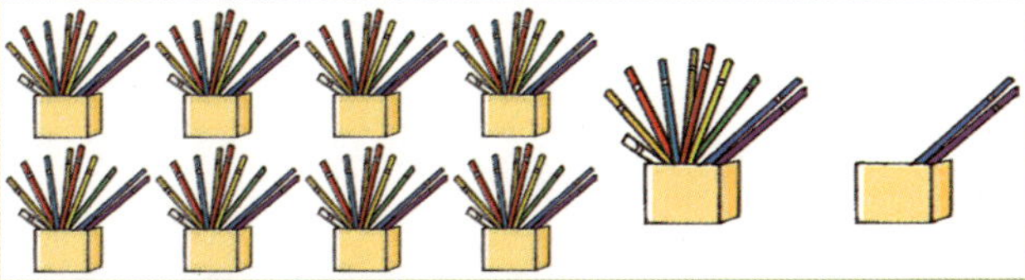	9 tens	2 ones	=	92	Ninety-two
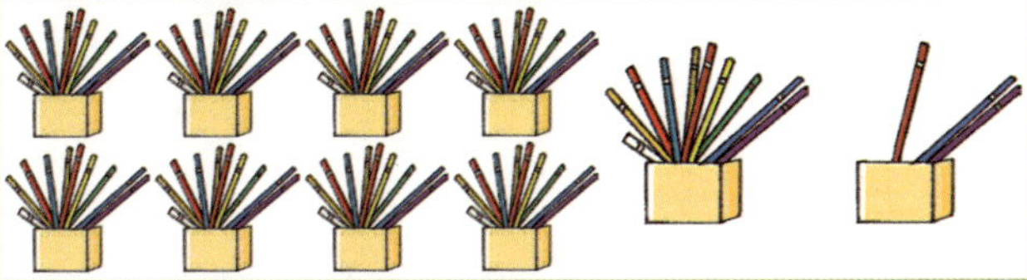	tens	ones	=	93	Ninety-three
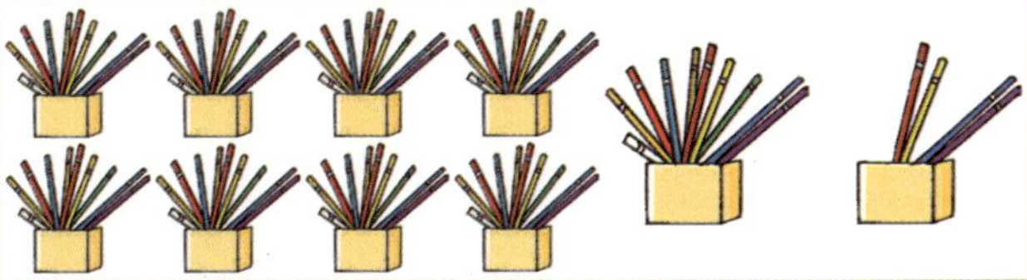	tens	ones	=	94	Ninety-four
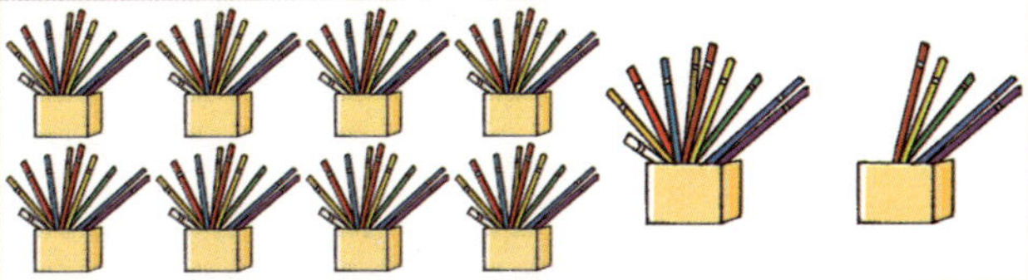	tens	ones	=	95	Ninety-five
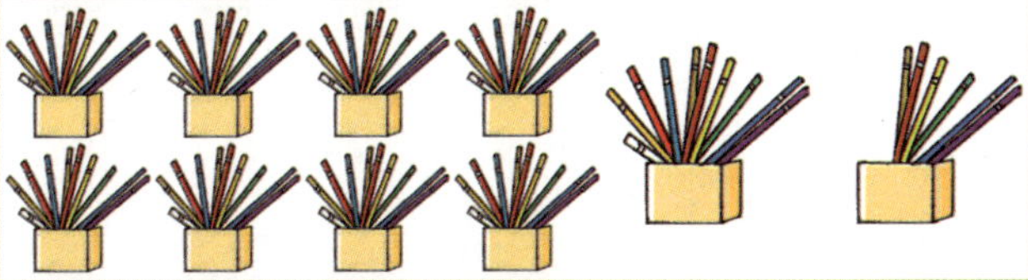	tens	ones	=	96	Ninety-six
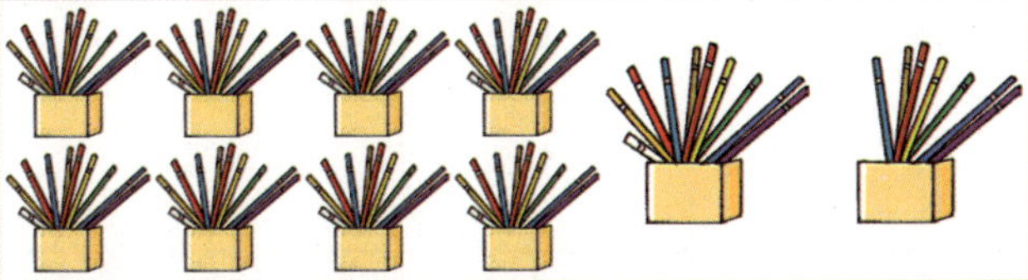	tens	ones	=	97	Ninety-seven
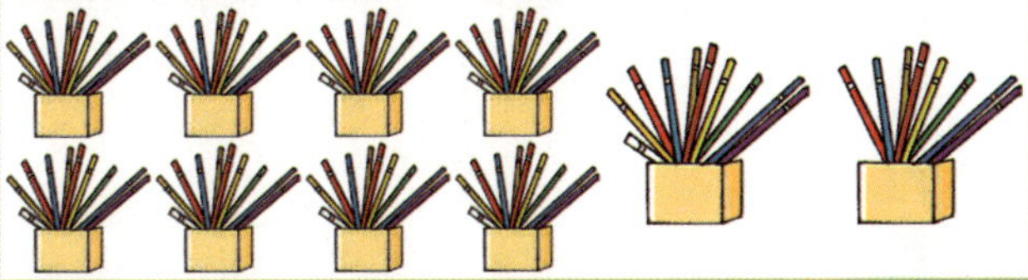	tens	ones	=	98	Ninety-eight
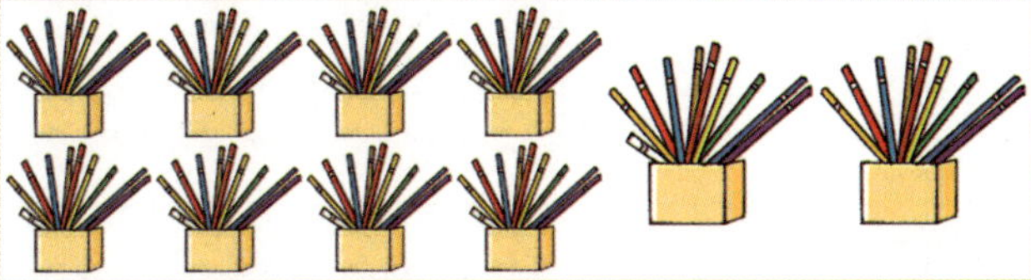	tens	ones	=	99	Ninety-nine
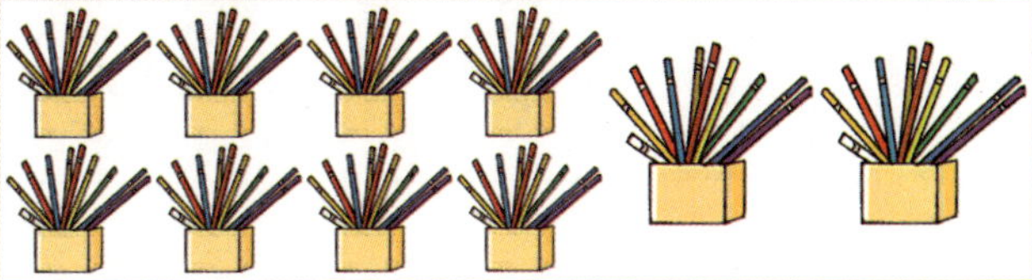	tens	ones	=	100	Hundred

Number Grid

Write counting 1-100 in the number grid given below.

1	2								
									100

Write the numbers

Forty-nine	
Seventy-six	
Eighty-three	
Thirty	
Sixty-six	
Fifty-five	
Thirteen	
Eighty-one	
Ninety-nine	
Fifty-eight	

Write numbers for the expanded form.

6 tens is ____

4 tens 3 ones is ____

2 tens 6 ones is ____

8 tens 1 ones is ____

5 tens 9 ones is ____

2 tens 2 ones is ____

Write the number name for these.

37		46	
19		89	
44		52	
98		71	
63		35	

Fill in the missing numbers

1									
									20
				25					
			34						
						47			
							58		
61									
								79	
	82								
		93							

Colour the correct number in pink.

Sixty-four	63	64	46	54
Forty-five	45	54	55	44
Fifty-nine	41	94	59	39
Seventy-one	79	17	71	97
Fifty	5	50	60	80
Ninety-seven	79	97	77	87
Twenty-nine	19	29	39	92
Eighty-six	86	98	68	89
Thirty-one	36	63	31	67

What comes before? Circle in red.

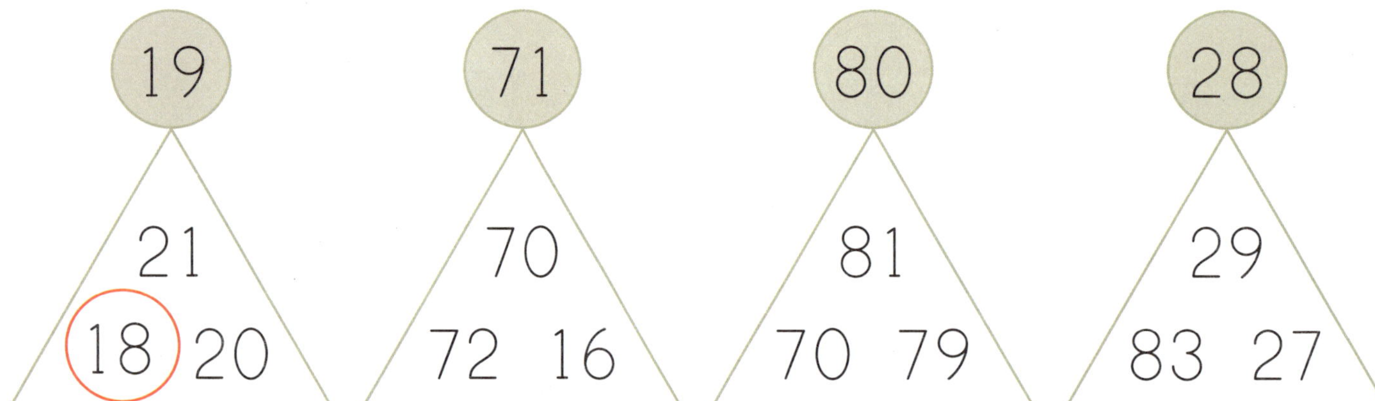

What comes after? Circle in green.

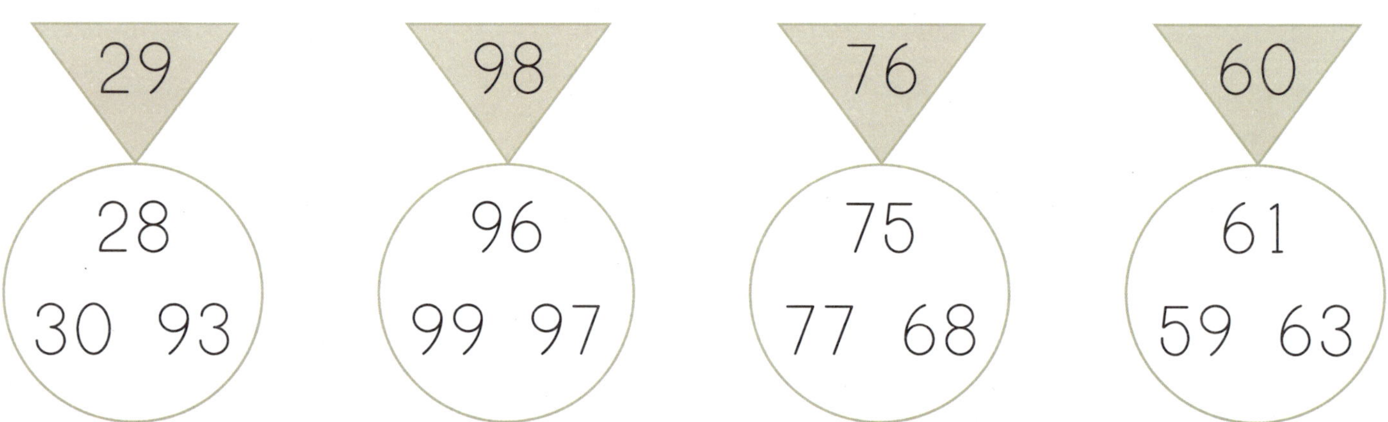

Count and write the number of objects.

	2 tens = 20
	tens =
	tens =
	tens =
	tens =
	tens =
	tens =
	tens =
	tens = 100

Count the balls and fill in the blanks with tens and ones.

	2 tens 0 ones = 20
	3 tens 3 ones = 33
	☐ tens ☐ ones = ☐
	☐ tens ☐ ones = ☐
	☐ tens ☐ ones = ☐
	☐ tens ☐ ones = ☐
	☐ tens ☐ ones = ☐
	☐ tens ☐ ones = ☐
	☐ tens ☐ ones = ☐

Fill in the blanks

tens	ones							
5	6	=	50	+	6	=	56
7	5	=	70	+	5	=	75
2	1	=		+		=	
3	0	=		+		=	
8	9	=		+		=	
6	4	=		+		=	
1	8	=		+		=	
6	9	=		+		=	
	5	=	40	+	5	=	

Draw beads on the abacus and show the numbers

T	O
4	6

T	O
3	9

T	O
8	0

T	O
2	5

T	O
7	2

T	O
6	4

T	O
5	1

T	O
9	9

Count the beads on the abacus and write the numbers

T	O

T	O

T	O

T	O

T	O

T	O

T	O

T	O

Expanded Form

Write in the expanded form

Number		Tens	Ones			+	
38	=	3 tens	8 ones	=	30	+	8
47	=	4 tens	7 ones	=		+	
56	=	tens	ones	=		+	
98	=	tens	ones	=		+	
20	=	tens	ones	=		+	
86	=	tens	ones	=		+	
63	=	tens	ones	=		+	

72 = ___ tens ___ ones = ___ + ___

14 = ___ tens ___ ones = ___ + ___

89 = ___ tens ___ ones = ___ + ___

90 = ___ tens ___ ones = ___ + ___

18 = ___ tens ___ ones = ___ + ___

42 = ___ tens ___ ones = ___ + ___

57 = ___ tens ___ ones = ___ + ___

45 = ___ tens ___ ones = ___ + ___

Comparing Numbers

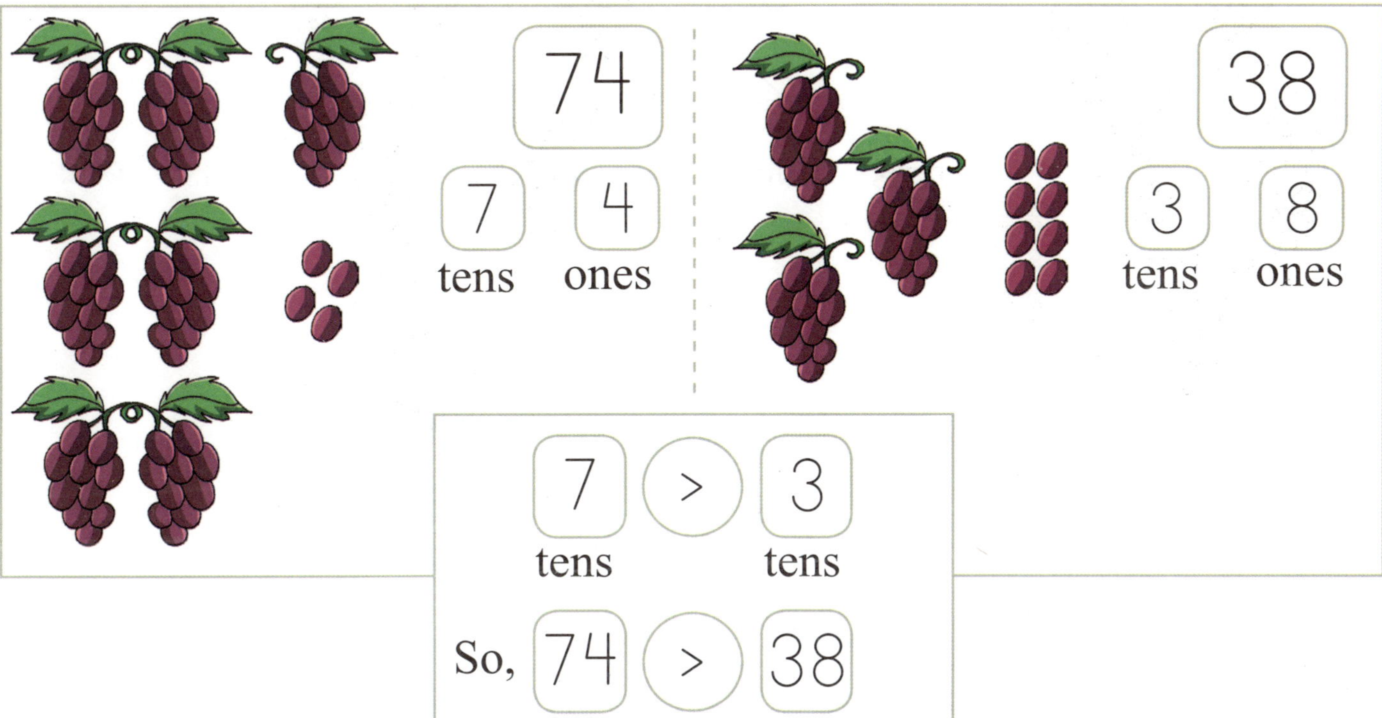

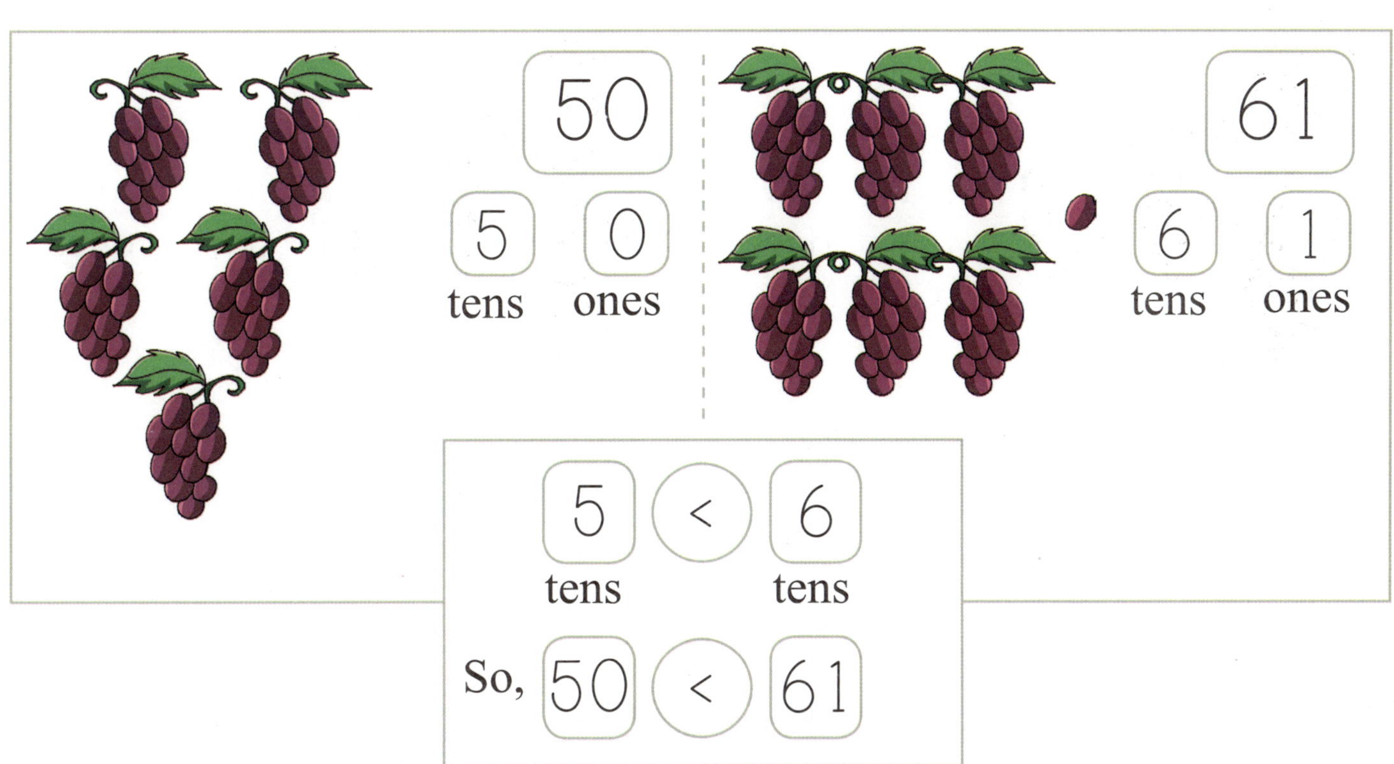

56

5 tens 6 ones

54

5 tens 4 ones

5 tens = 5 tens

6 ones > 4 ones

So, 56 > 54

35

3 tens 5 ones

35

3 tens 5 ones

3 tens = 3 tens

5 ones = 5 ones

35 = 35

Compare the numbers and insert the correct sign (>, <, =).

66 ◯ 77	41 ◯ 81	79 ◯ 81
59 ◯ 85	27 ◯ 72	68 ◯ 69
68 ◯ 86	50 ◯ 39	30 ◯ 48
39 ◯ 38	21 ◯ 12	77 ◯ 66
50 ◯ 41	84 ◯ 91	60 ◯ 82

Write > < in the blanks below

Fifty-three	◯	Fifty-nine
Sixty-five	◯	Twenty-nine
Ninety	◯	Eighty-nine
Thirty-five	◯	Thirty-eight
Forty	◯	Twenty-three
Twenty-two	◯	Forty-two

Largest & Smallest

32	78	19	91

19 < 32

19 < 78

19 < 91

19 is the smallest in this group

91 > 32

91 > 78

91 > 19

91 is the largest in this group

While counting, the smallest number comes first. The largest number comes after the other numbers.

Circle the smallest number from each group in blue.

58	85	35	53	86
42	12	21	24	13
86	82	96	61	51

Circle the largest number from each group in red.

66	77	55	22
89	9	8	98
27	25	38	39

Addition and Subtraction (1-100)

11

Addition of Tens and Ones

Add and write in the ☐ provided.

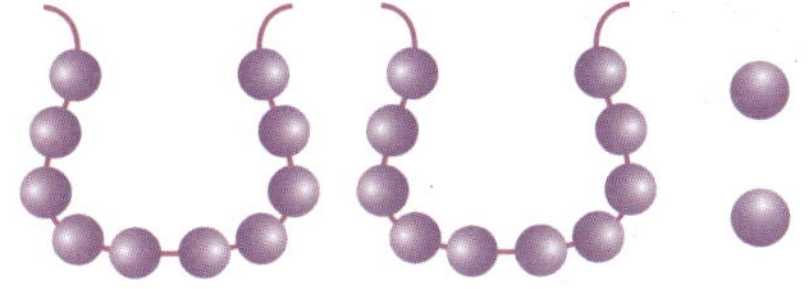

20 + 2 = ☐

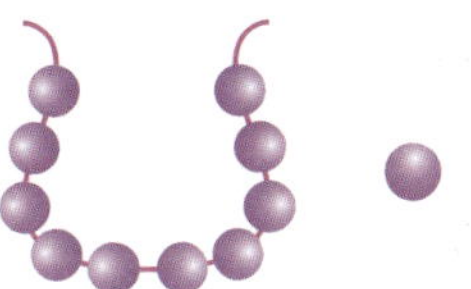

10 + 1 = ☐

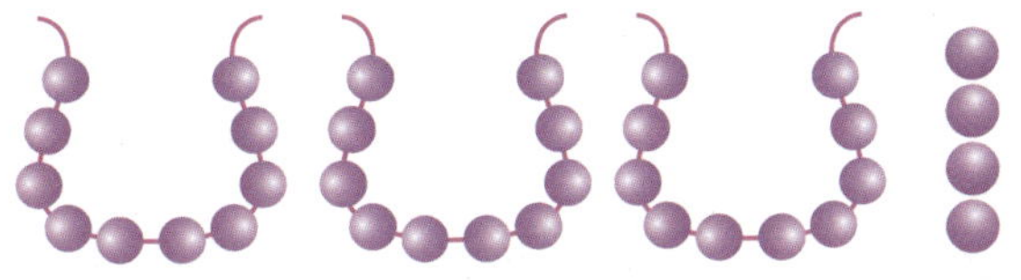

30 + 4 = ☐

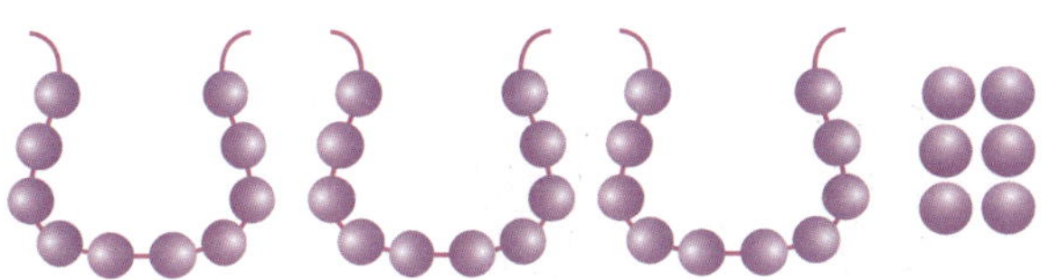

30 + 6 = ☐

10 + 0 = ☐

50 + 2 = ☐

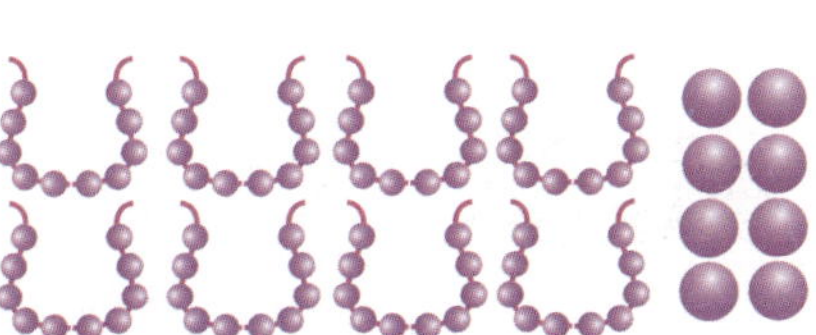

80 + 8 = ☐

☐ + 6 = ☐

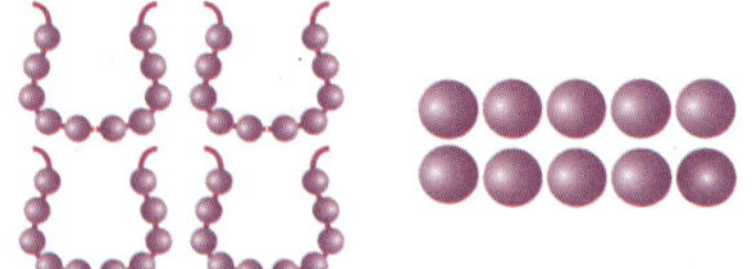

☐ + ☐ = ☐

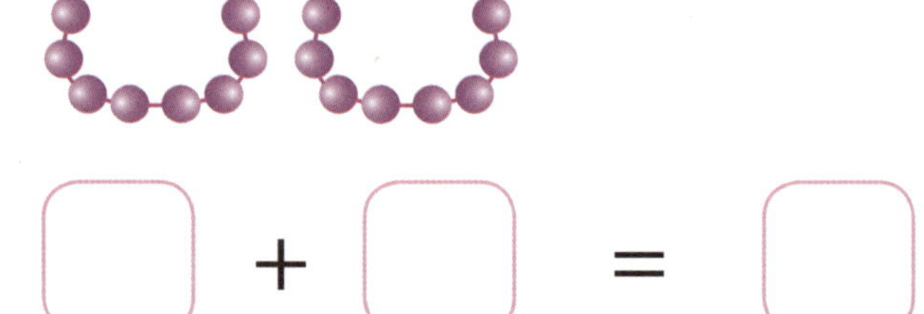

☐ + ☐ = ☐

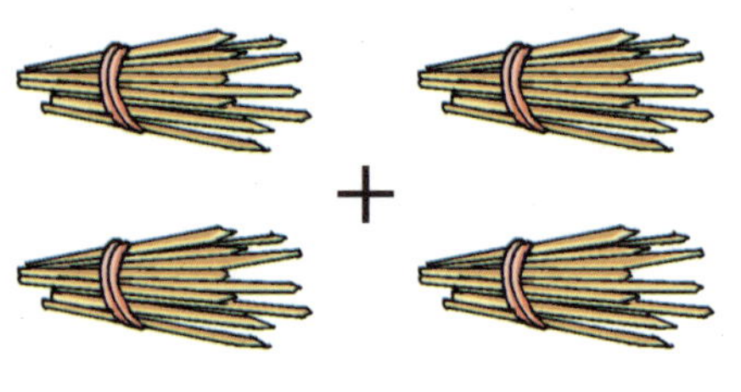

T	O
2	0
+2	0

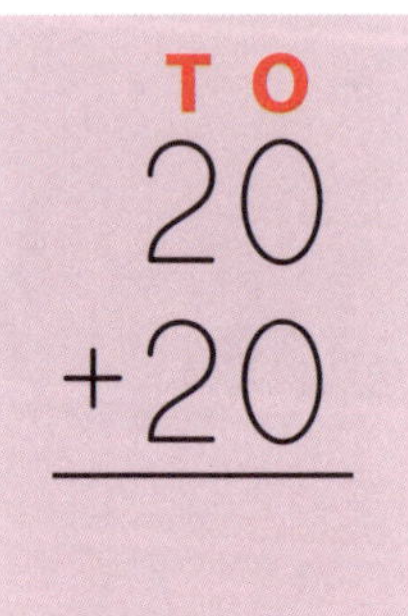

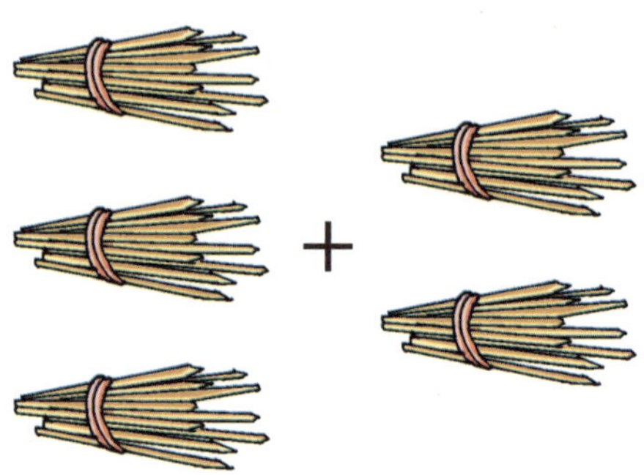

T	O
3	0
+2	0

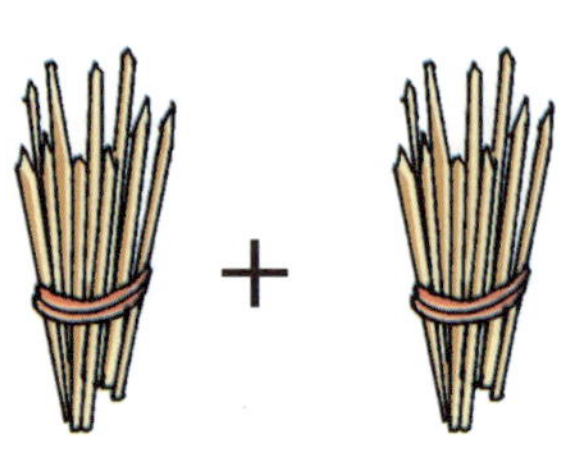

T	O
1	0
+1	0

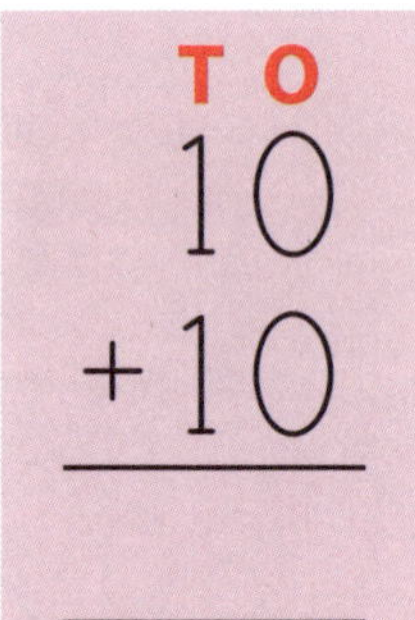

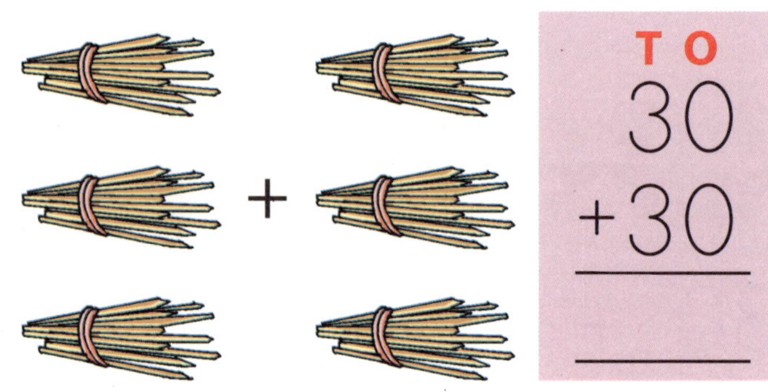

T	O
3	0
+3	0

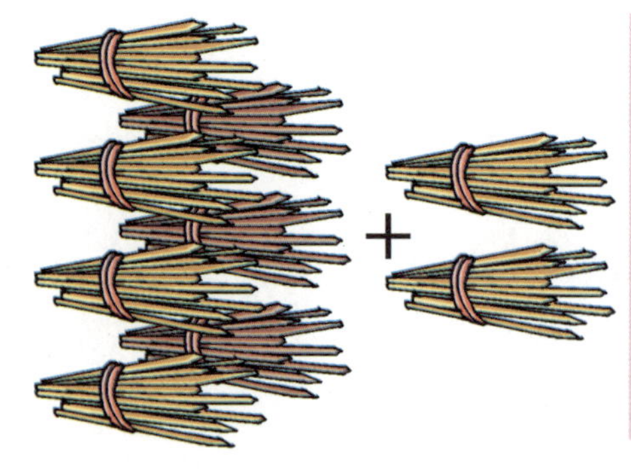

T	O
7	0
+2	0

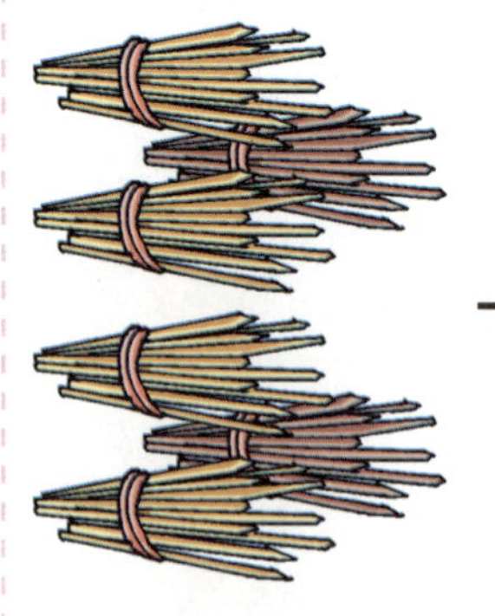

T	O
6	0
+1	0

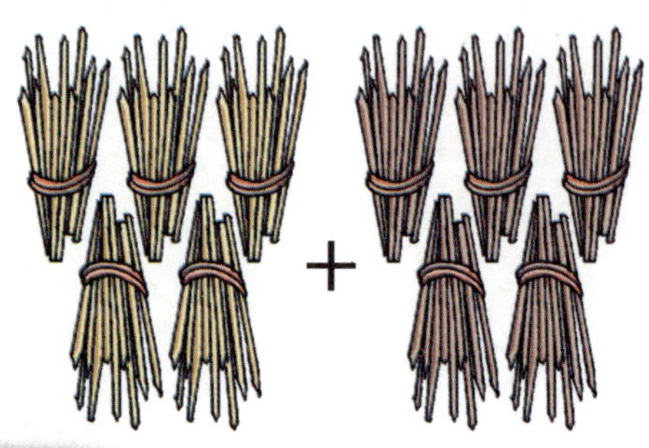

T	O
5	0
+5	0

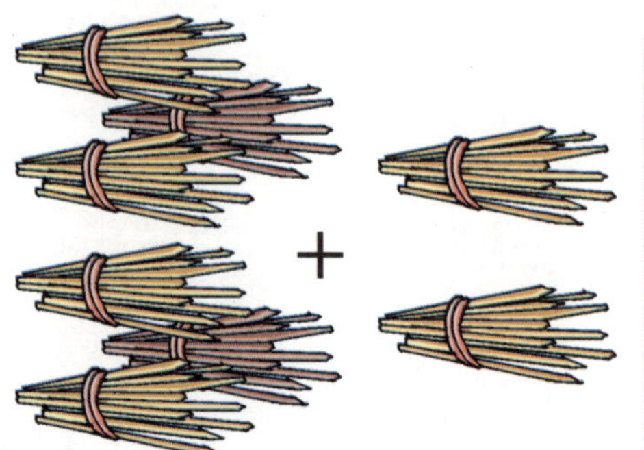

T	O
6	0
+2	0

Activity

The teacher can divide the class into groups of 3 or 4 students. They are given objects like ice cream sticks, buttons, beads, pencils. They are asked to count the objects they have. Students should be encouraged to put the objects in bunches/piles of 10.

Then the following sums should be given.

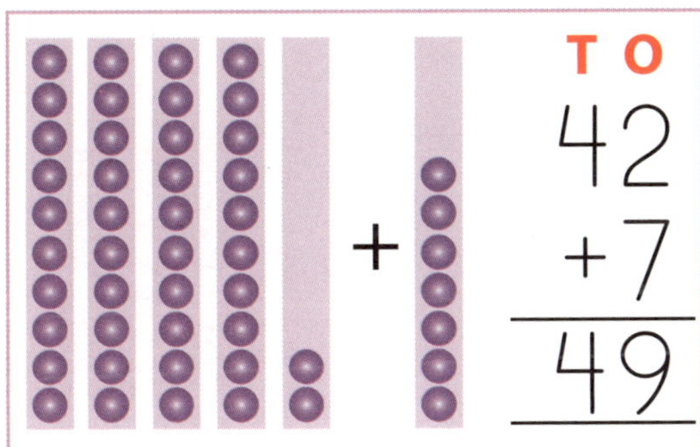

	T	O
	4	2
+		7
	4	9

Step 1: Put numbers in proper columns

Step 2: First add the ones

Step 3: Then add the tens

So, numbers can be written under tens and ones and then added.

T O	T O	T O	T O	T O
31	54	43	90	33
+2	+5	+6	+9	+3
____	____	____	____	____

T O	T O	T O	T O
51	41	77	35
+5	+8	+2	+4
____	____	____	____

Teacher should draw the attention of students to the fact that ones are added to ones and tens with tens.

Additions (2-Digit Numbers)

T O	T O	T O	T O	T O
44	73	23	61	32
+33	+14	+14	+17	+45

T O	T O	T O	T O	T O
54	80	62	58	22
+15	+19	+14	+31	+55

T O	T O	T O	T O	T O
33	49	13	41	75
+23	+20	+14	+57	+11

T O	T O	T O	T O	T O
27	82	71	32	26
+11	+16	+17	+24	+52

Word Problems

Arthur had 42 sweets. His Mother gave him 6 more.
How many sweets does Arthur have now?

T	O
4	2
+	6
4	8

Total sweets

Beck has 34 comics. His Uncle gifts him 5 more.
How many does he have altogether?

T	O
3	4
+	5

Total comics

In a class there are 18 boys and 21 girls.
How many students in all?

T	O

Total students

A fruit seller has 40 mangoes and 58 bananas.
What is the total number of fruits?

T	O

Total fruits

Subtraction (1–99)

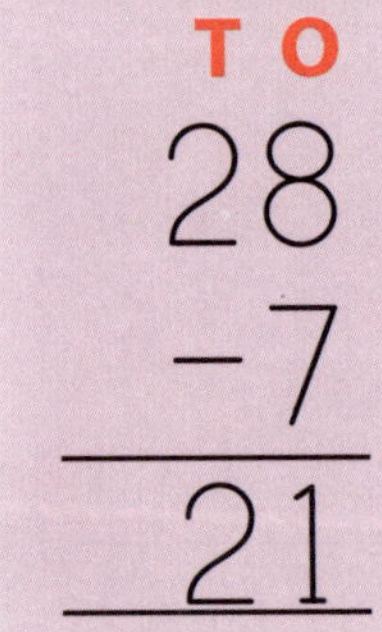

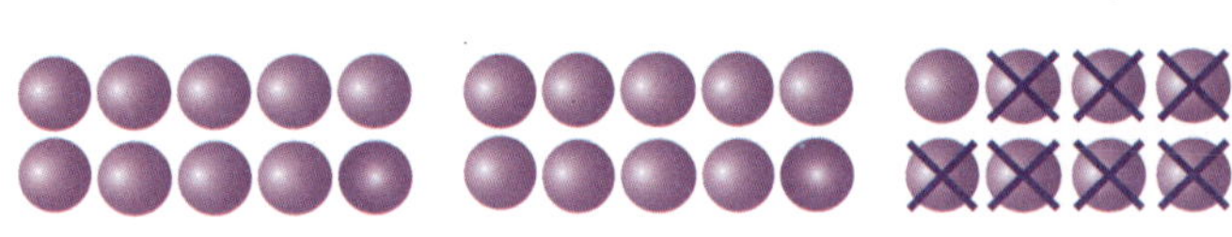

Out of 28 marbles 7 are crossed out. Remaining numbers of marbles is 21.

Draw string of beads or boxes of marbles or bundles of sticks to fill in the boxes.

T O
36
−15
21

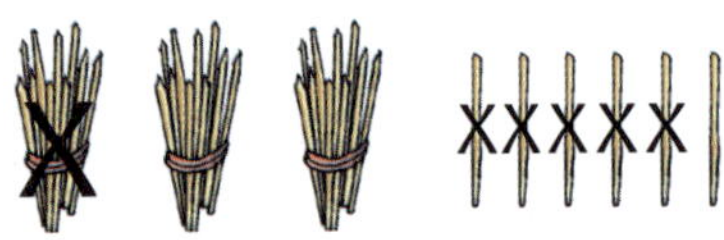

T O
49
−29

T O
78
−43

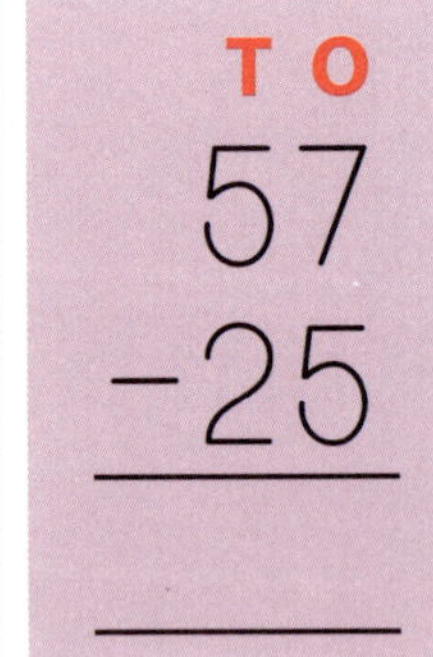

T O
84
−32

T O
29
−3

Subtraction of Tens and Ones

Subtract the ones and write under 'ones'. Subtract the tens and write under 'tens'.

T O	T O	T O	T O	T O
48	34	79	86	57
−37	−14	−31	−55	−32
___	___	___	___	___

T O	T O	T O	T O	T O
62	43	77	89	39
−20	−23	−44	−29	−27
___	___	___	___	___

T O	T O	T O	T O	T O
85	66	92	58	49
−31	−33	−50	−16	−19
___	___	___	___	___

T O	T O	T O	T O	T O
68	37	48	56	79
−25	−14	−35	−40	−38
___	___	___	___	___

Word Problems

In a shop there are 48 cups. 17 cups break. How many are left?

T O
48
−17

Cups left ______

There are 88 birds on a tree. 36 birds fly away. How many birds are left?

T O
88
−36

Birds left ______

Peter has 95 candies. He gives 74 candies to his friends. How many candies are left with Peter?

T O

Candies left ______

A book has 85 pages. Rita read 64 pages. How many pages are left?

T O

Pages left ______

REVIEW EXERCISE 3

Fill in the boxes

7 tens + 8 ones = ☐

3 tens + 0 ones = ☐

6 tens + 6 ones = ☐

4 tens + 1 ones = ☐

6 tens + 2 ones = ☐

Write the number names.

30 = ☐

84 = ☐

96 = ☐

42 = ☐

Fill in the boxes

40 + 20 = ☐

60 + 5 = ☐

80 + 10 = ☐

30 + 9 = ☐

Addition

T O	T O	T O	T O
33 +6 ____	80 +11 ____	92 +5 ____	66 +30 ____

T O	T O	T O	T O
44 +55 ____	64 +23 ____	35 +14 ____	70 +27 ____

Fill in '>' or '<' in the space provided.

78 ◯ 87

38  31

41 ◯ 51

19 ◯ 91

48  38

67 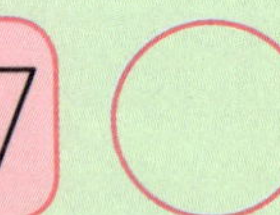 58

What comes between?

78  

69  71

38  

50  52

77  79

Addition of 3 Numbers

12

Add with the help of the number line.

$2 + 3 + 4 =$ 9

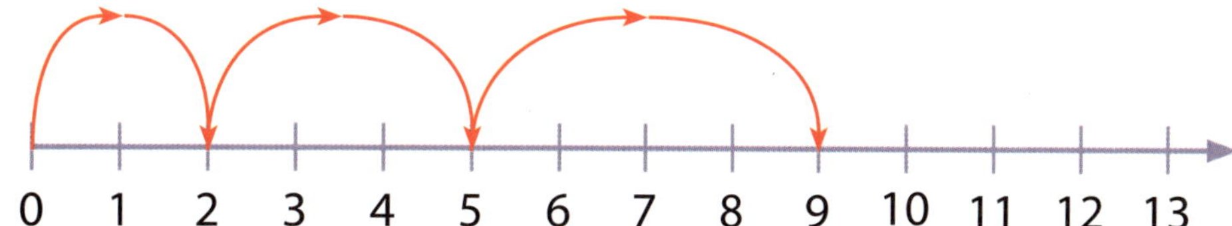

$3 + 3 + 4 =$ ☐

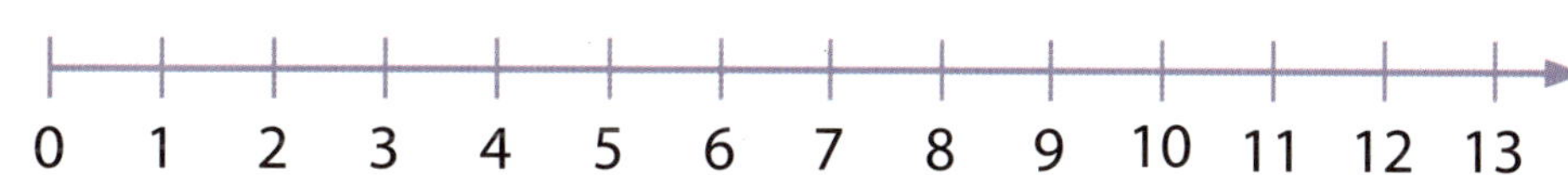

$5 + 4 + 3 =$ ☐

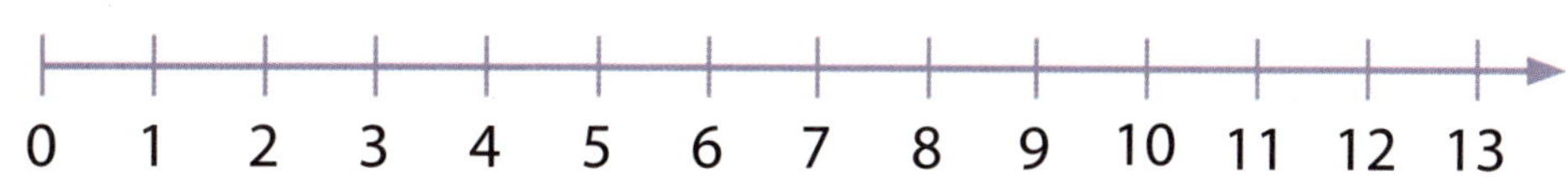

$4 + 4 + 4 =$ ☐

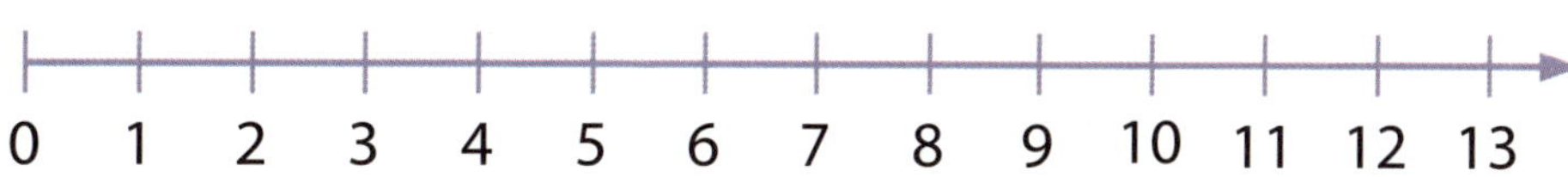

$6 + 3 + 4 =$ ☐

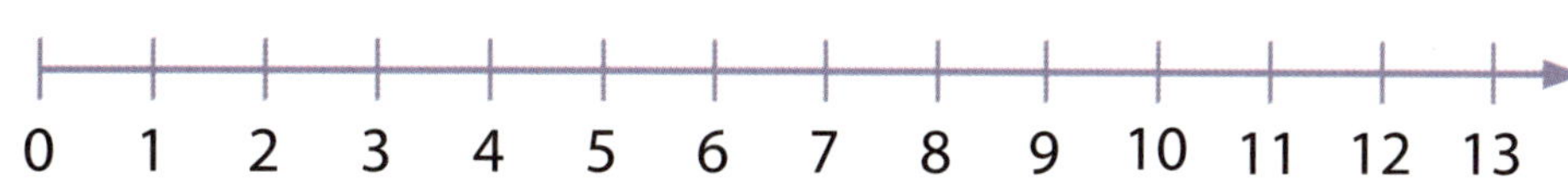

$1 + 4 + 0 =$ ☐

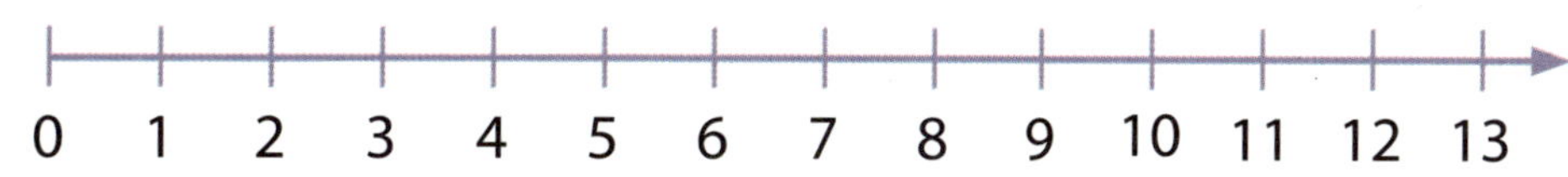

$5 + 5 + 3 =$ ☐

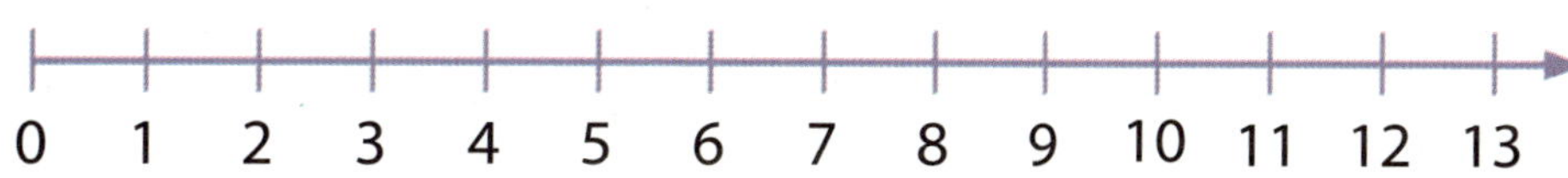

Add vertically

T O	T O	T O	T O	T O
4	5	6	4	5
3	1	4	4	5
+2	+2	+3	+4	+6

T O	T O	T O	T O	T O
1	7	8	5	10
4	0	3	23	20
+6	+5	+4	+41	+30

T O	T O	T O	T O	T O
19	73	44	56	4
30	2	23	12	3
+50	+4	+12	+20	+21

T O	T O	T O	T O	T O
30	75	51	22	64
60	13	16	33	21
+5	+11	+22	+44	+12

Patterns

Carry on the pattern

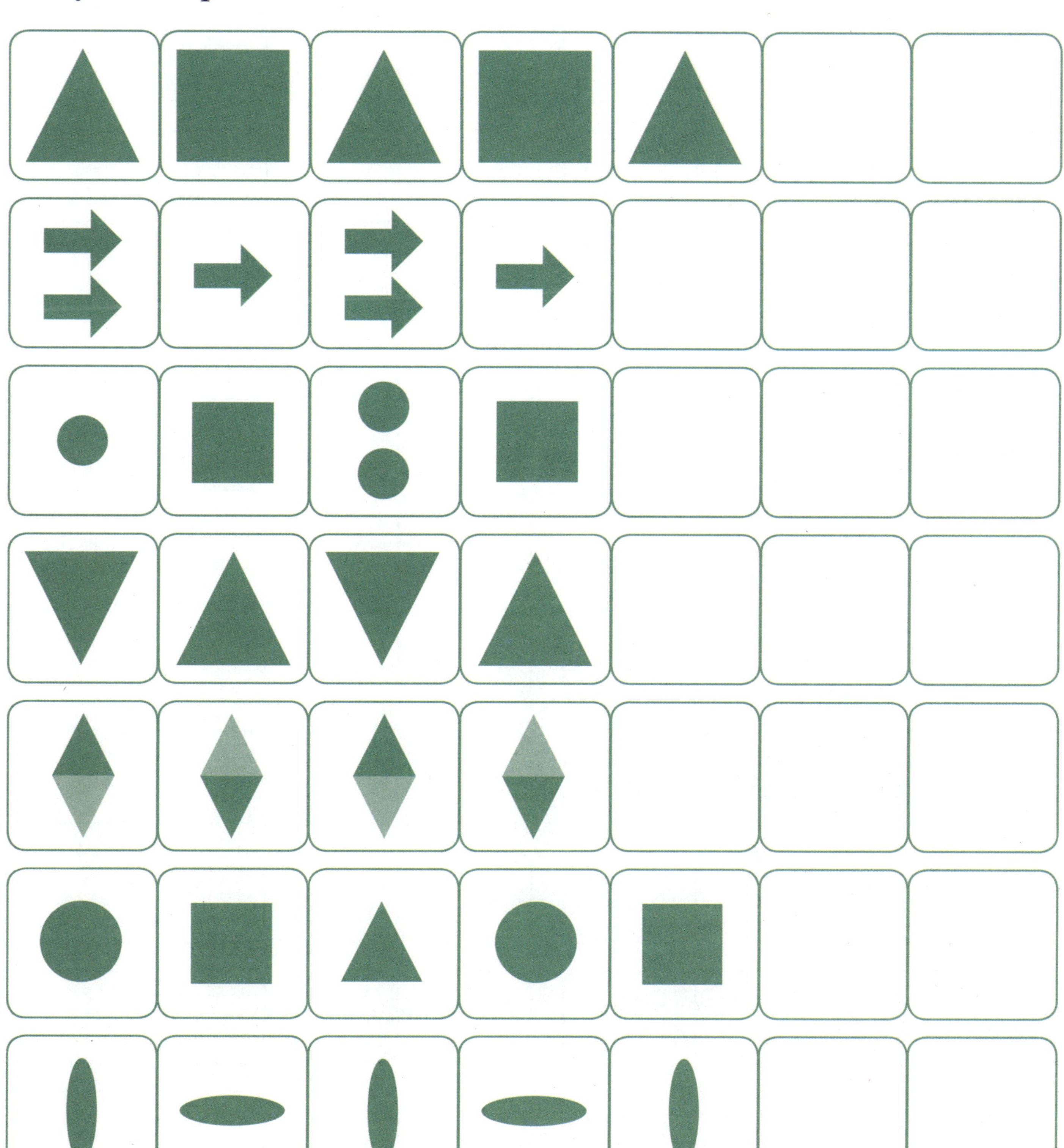

Observe the pattern and fill the boxes.

2	4	6	8				
1	3	5	7				
10	20	30	40				
23	24	25	26				
68	70	72	74				
20	19	18	17				
10	9	8	7				
30	27	24	21				
75	76	77	78				
80	82	84	86				
52	54	56	58				

Geometry

14

Shapes

The shapes we see around us.

Flat Shapes

Circle

Cent

Disk

Triangle

Triangle

Ice cream

Flag

Rectangle

Rectangle

Book cover

Square

Square paper piece

Kite

Group Activity

Things needed: carrot, coin, eraser, lady finger, capsicum, paint, powder

How to do the activity

Take pieces of carrot, lady finger, capsicum, sliced in different ways. Dip the flat side in paint and then press them on a sheet of paper. You get many shapes. Press the flat surfaces of erasers and coins in powder. Then press on coloured paper. You get different shapes.

Join dots to make shapes

Match the objects with the correct shapes.

Objects **Shapes**

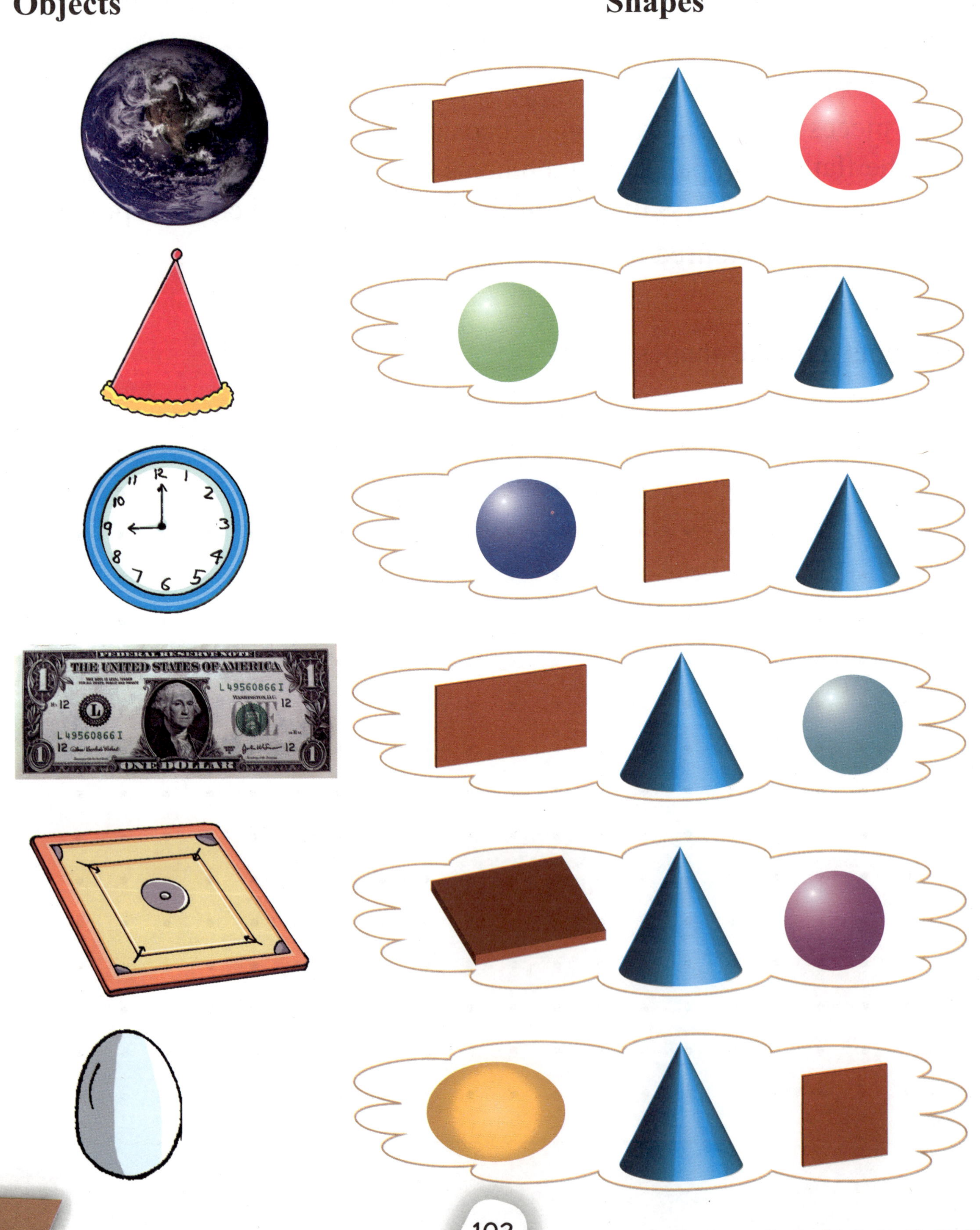

Complete the names of the basic shapes.

T _ _ _ _ _ _ E

S _ _ A _ _

R _ _ _ A _ _ _ _

_ _ _ C _ _

Draw objects that will roll down

Pick from the box

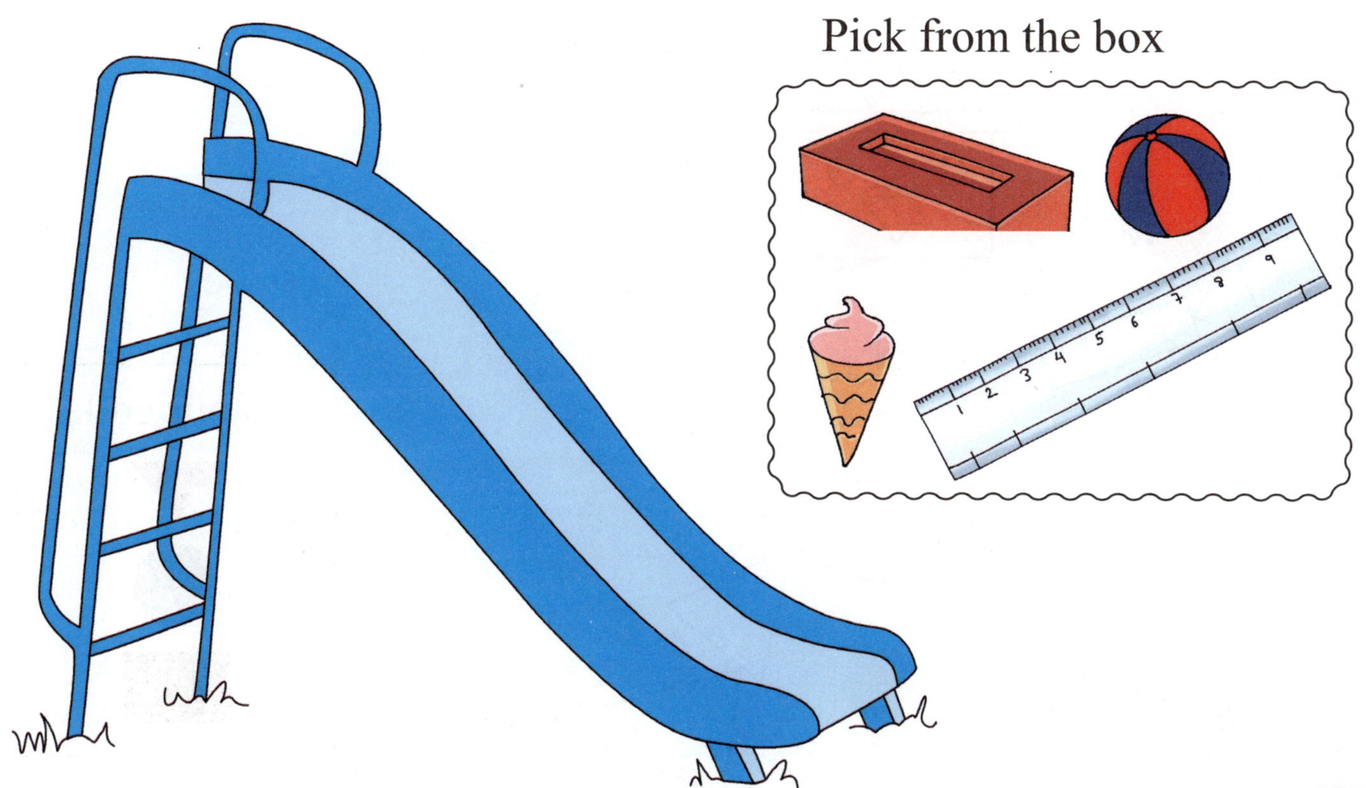

Circle the number of sides in the shapes given below.

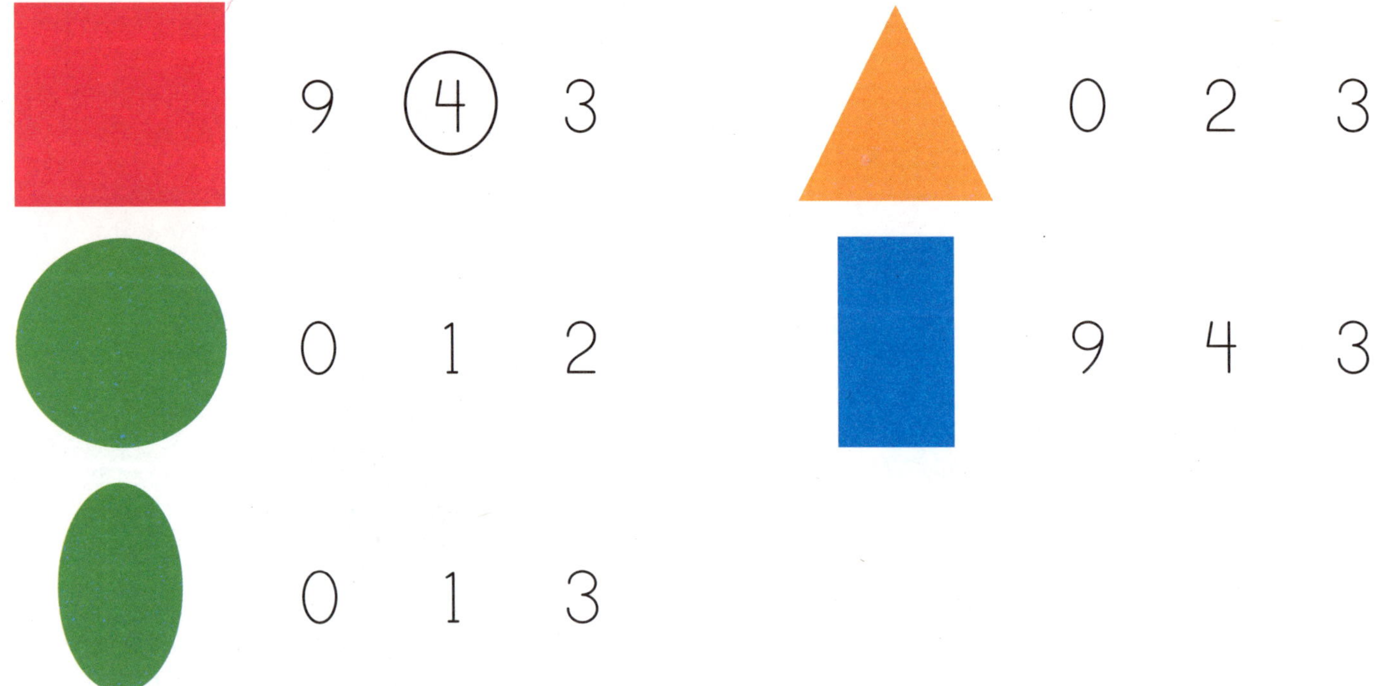

See the picture, count and write the number of triangles, circles and rectangles.

Colour the triangles red, circles blue and rectangles brown.

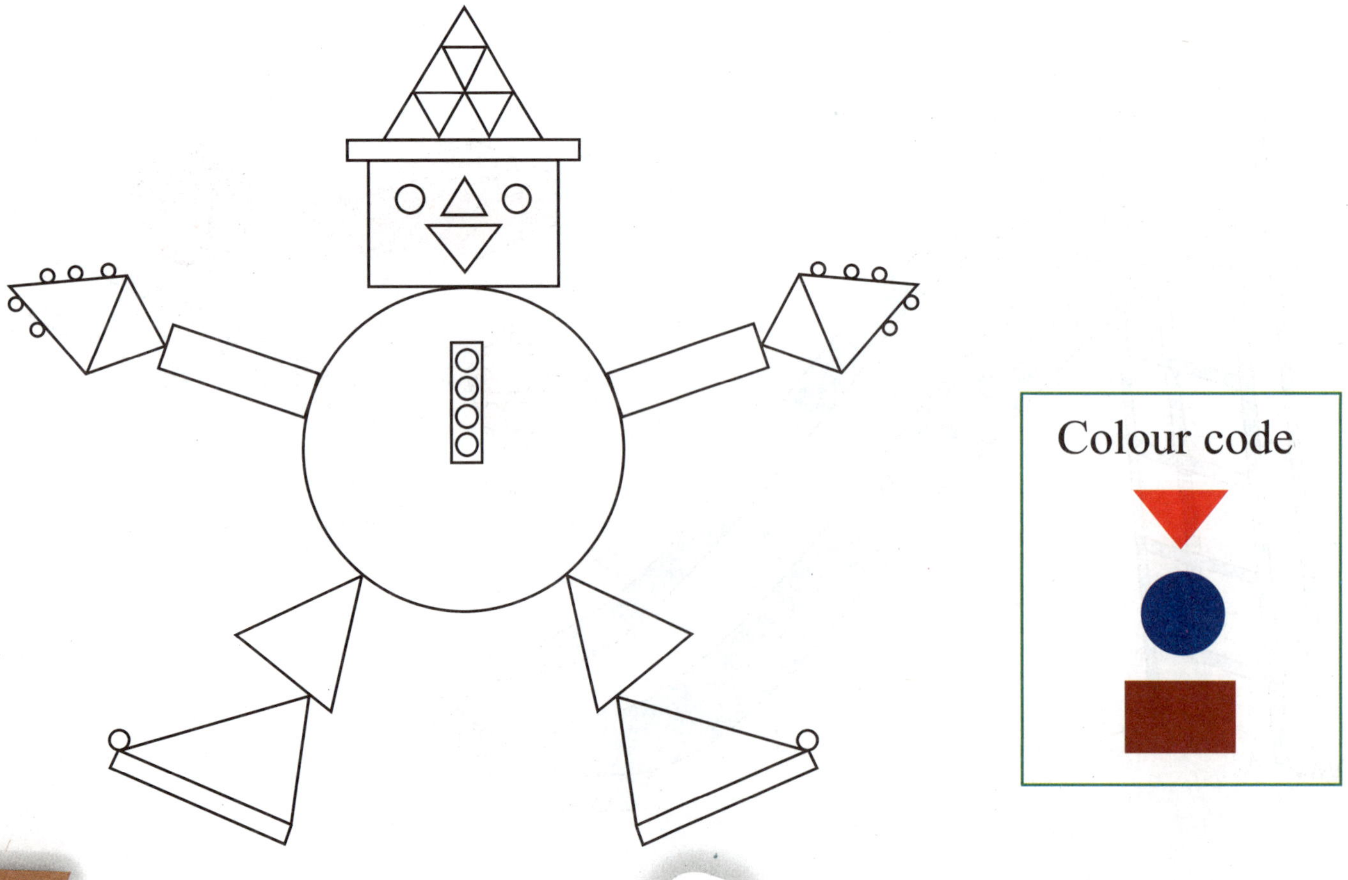

15 Measurement

The pen is longer than the pencil

The book is 2 pencils long

When we need to know how long a thing is, we can use different parts of our body to measure it. We can use hand span, cubit, foot span or a foot stride.

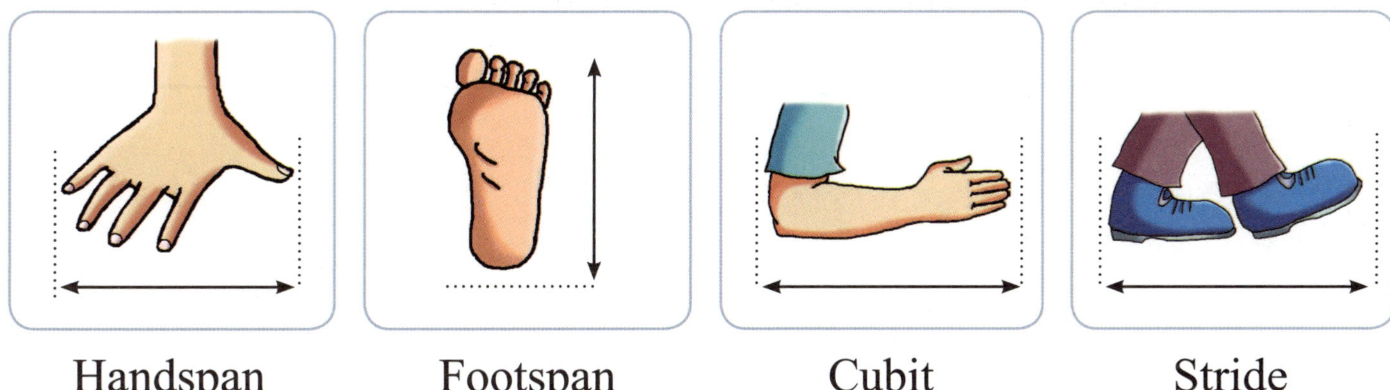

Handspan Footspan Cubit Stride

1. The desk is __________ hand spans long.
2. The room is __________ foot spans long.
3. Teacher's table is __________ foot strides away.
4. The door is ___________ away.

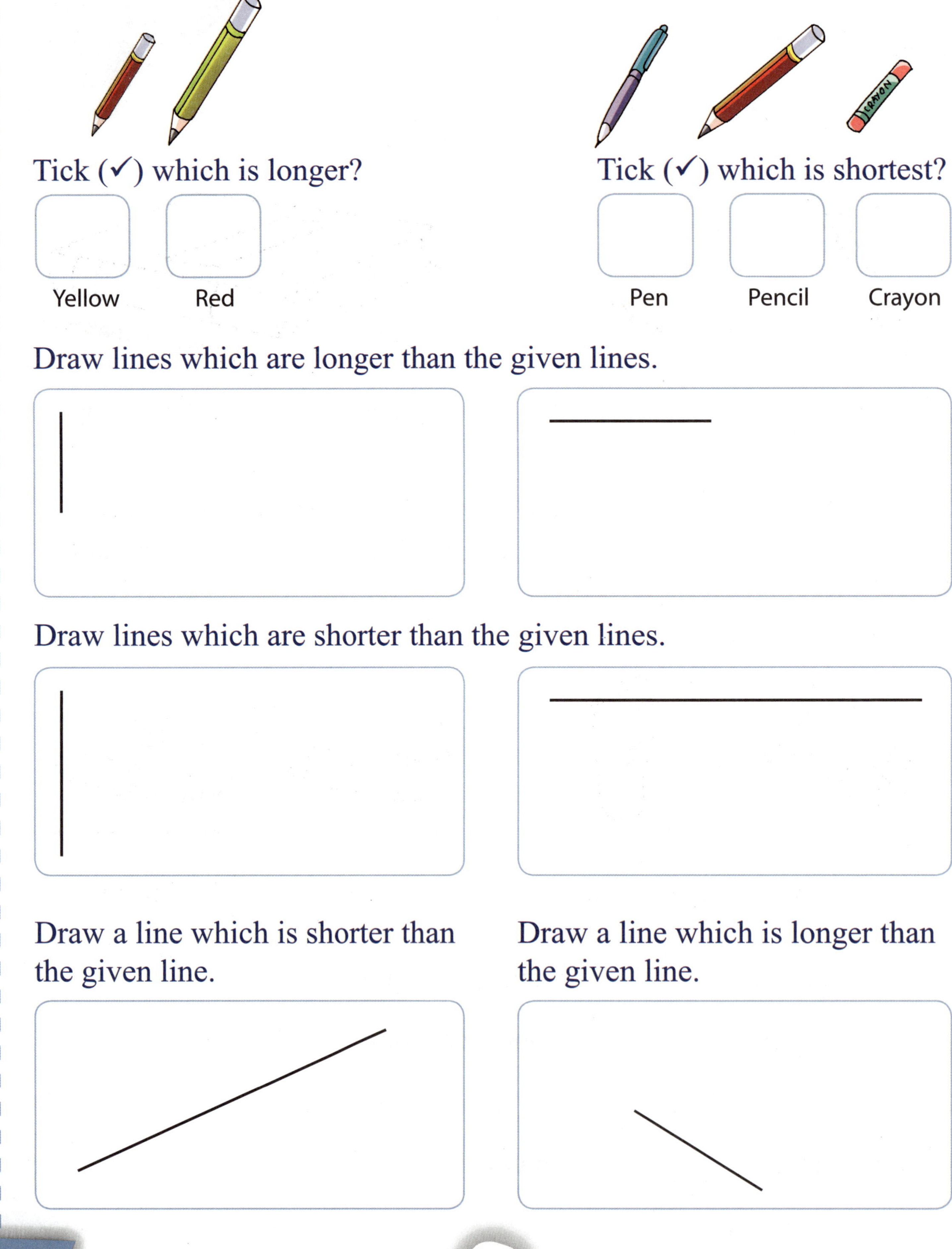

Tick (✓) which is longer?

Yellow Red

Tick (✓) which is shortest?

Pen Pencil Crayon

Draw lines which are longer than the given lines.

Draw lines which are shorter than the given lines.

Draw a line which is shorter than the given line.

Draw a line which is longer than the given line.

Lab Activity

Aim: To use different measuring tools.

Things we need: A sheet of square paper

How to do: Cut a strip of square paper and number the boxes as shown below. Use it for measuring.

1	2	3	4	5	6	7	8	9	10	11	12	13	14	15

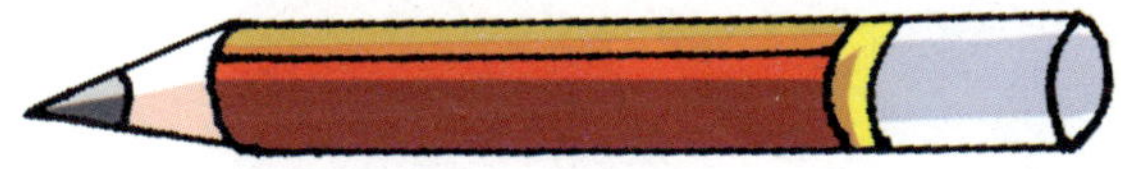

The pencil is 6 boxes long.

	Pencil	Pen	Pencil box	Maths book	Index finger
Student 1					
Student 2					

Are the measurements using the strip the same?

Can you think of any other tool?

Scale/Rulers are also like the measuring strip.

1 2 3 4 5 6 7 8 9 10 11 12

1 2 3 4 5

Teacher mentions non uniform tools of measurement.

Time

16

Clocks and watches tell us the time.

When the sun rises it is day.

Day

After sunset, it is dark. Night falls.

Night

In the clocks, the short hand is the hour-hand. The long hand shows minutes. It is called minute-hand.

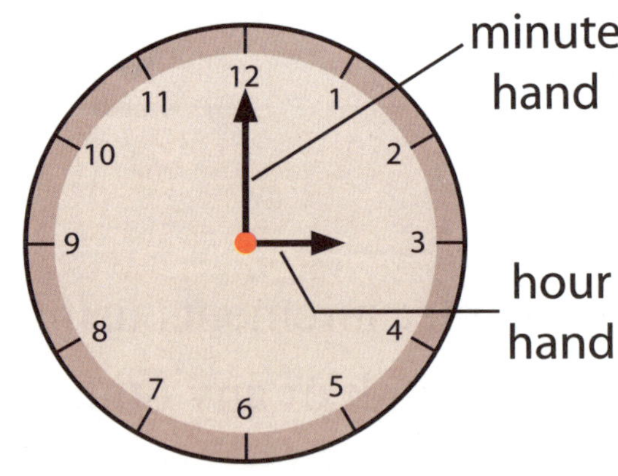

[It is 3 0' clock or 3:00]

It is 8 o'clock or 8:00

It is ________ or ________

It is ________ or ________

It is ________ or ________

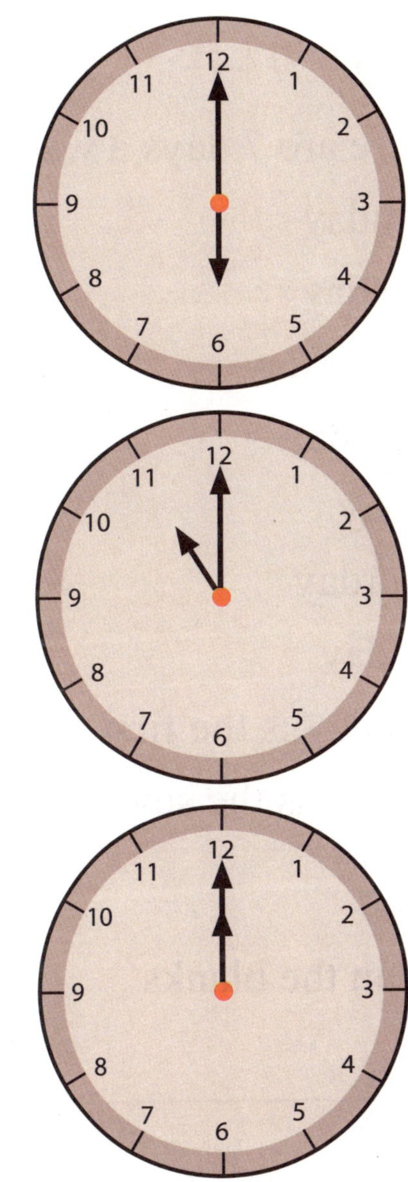

Look at the pictures and write the time in the boxes below.

Days of a Week

There are 7 days a week.

Monday

Tuesday

Wednesday

Thursday

Friday

Saturday

Sunday

Monday is the first day.

Sunday is the seventh day.

JANUARY						
Sun	Mon	Tue	Wed	Thu	Fri	Sat
						1
2	3	4	5	6	7	8
9	10	11	12	13	14	15
16	17	18	19	20	21	22
23	24	25	26	27	28	29
30	31					

Fill in the blanks

1. ______________________ is the first day of the week.

2. The second day of the week is ___________________

3. Wednesday comes after _________________________

4. Friday comes before ____________________________

5. ____________________________ comes after Sunday.

Lab Activity

The teacher gives the students a cut -out of a round clock with numbers marked from 1 to 12 and moveable hands.

Students draw the hour hand to show their daily routine.

Draw the hands of the clocks and fill in the blanks according to the clues given.

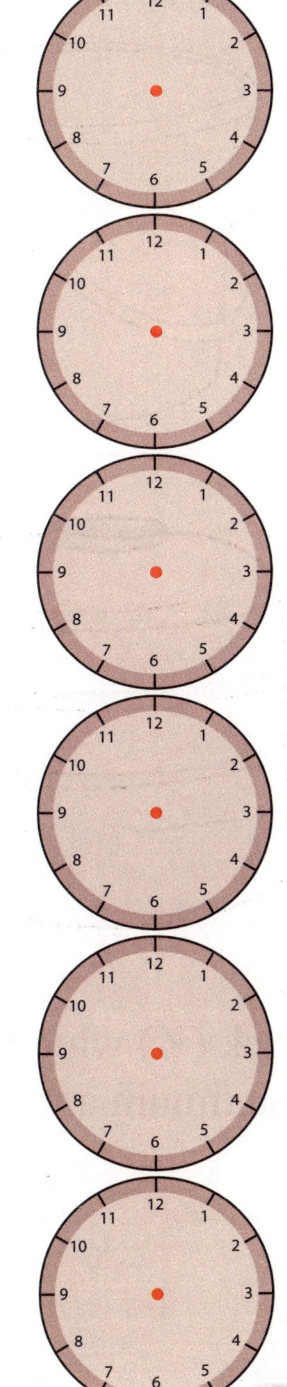

1. I get up at ________________

2. I go to school at ________________

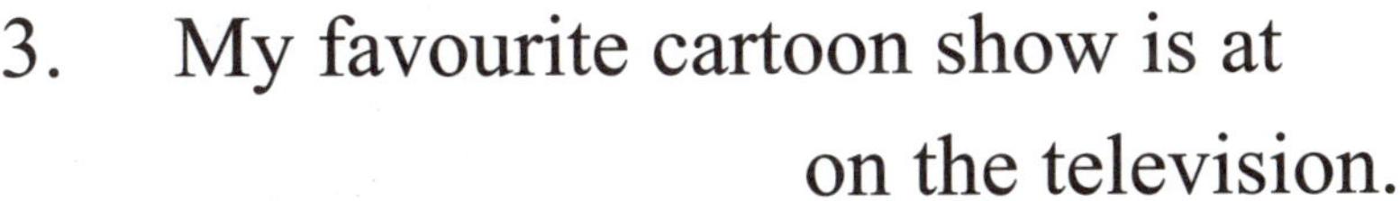

3. My favourite cartoon show is at ________________ on the television.

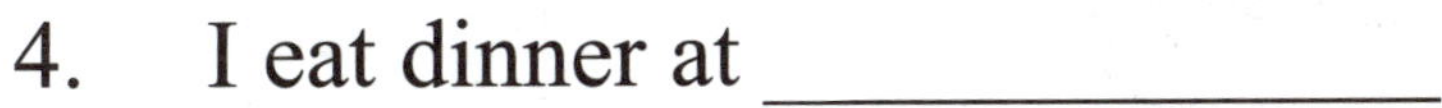

4. I eat dinner at ________________

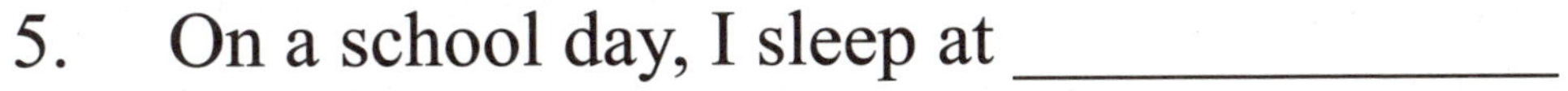

5. On a school day, I sleep at ________________

6. During holidays, I sleep late, at ______________

Capacity

17

Capacity is the amount of water (or any liquid) a container can hold. Big containers hold more liquids. Their **capacity** is more.

Colour the container that can hold more water in blue.

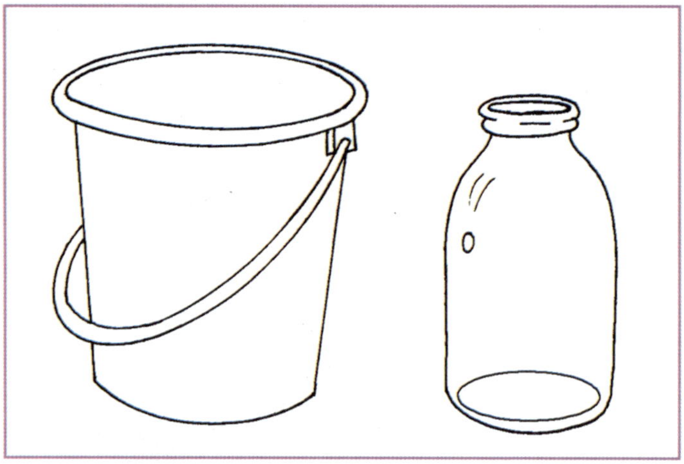

A  B 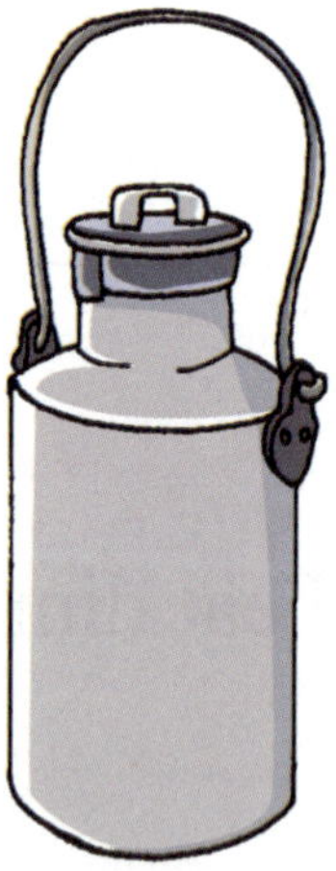 C

Tick (✓) which container holds maximum amount of water?

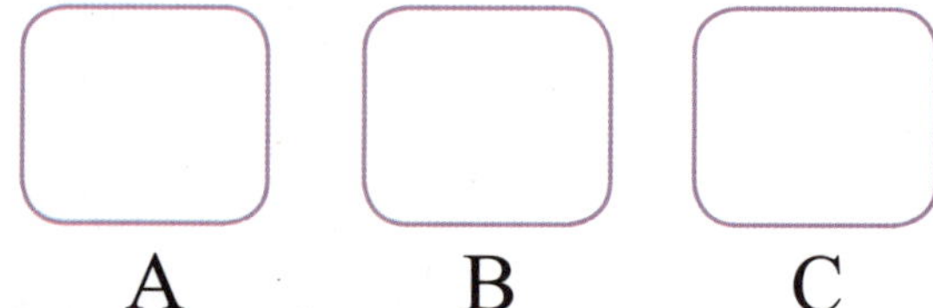

Tick (✓) which container holds the least amount of water?

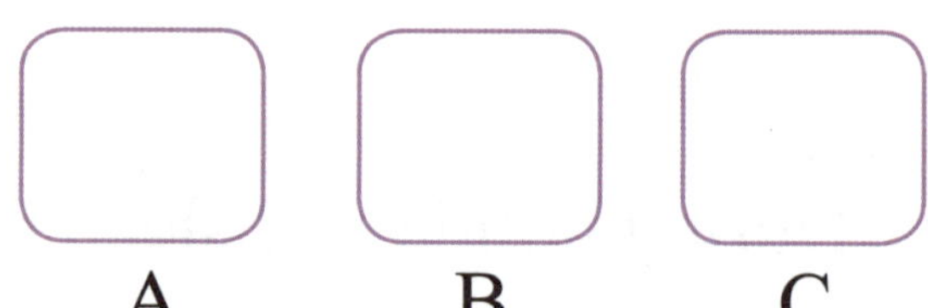

Lab Activity

Take a water bottle and let the child fill it with a cup.

Use the same cup to fill water bottles of other children.

	WATER BOTTLE OF	CAPACITY
	Ronny	4 cups
	Mira	
	Daniel	

Draw 2 containers which have more capacity than the bucket

Draw 2 containers which have less capacity than the cup.

Weight

Weight of an object means how heavy or light it is.

This bag is heavy

This bag is light.

Colour the heavy object blue.

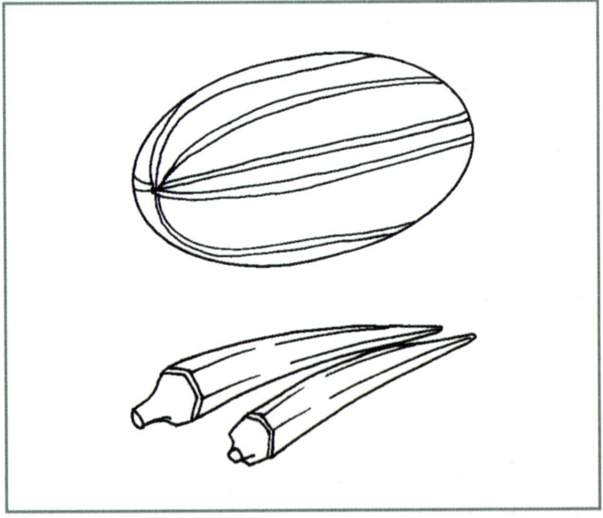

Colour the heavier boy red.

Draw 1 object heavier than the given object.

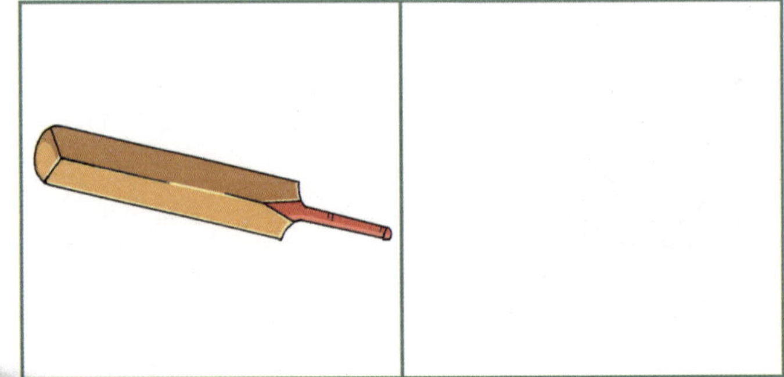

A 'Balance'

We use a 'balance' to measure weight. A balance has two pans.

The pan with heavier weight goes down

The pan with lighter weight goes up

Look at the balances and tick (✓) the heavier objects.

Look at the balances and cross (×) the lighter objects.

Money

19

We use money to buy things. In the US, it is in the form of dollars and cents. Given below are some cents and dollars.

1¢

5¢

10¢

25¢

50¢

$1

$1 = 100 cents

A cent has 2 sides - obverse and reverse

$1

=

100 cents

$2

=

100 cents

100 cents

The cost of some items is given below.

How much will a ball and a doll cost together?

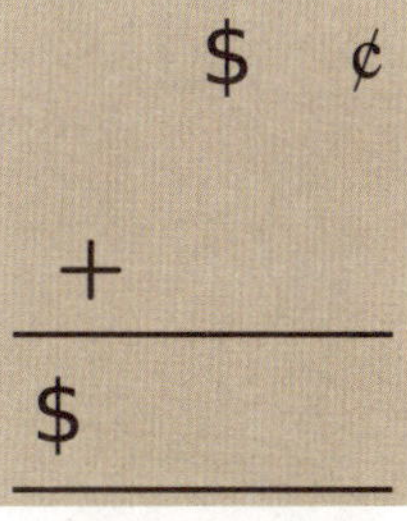

How much will a book and pencil cost together?

$ ¢

+

$

How much will a pen and a book cost together?

$ ¢

\+

$

How much money is needed to buy one pen, one ice cream and one packet of chips?

$ ¢

\+

$

You have $ 20. Can you buy a book and a cake?

$ ¢

\+

$

You have $ 15. You buy a bunch of balloons. How much money is left with you?

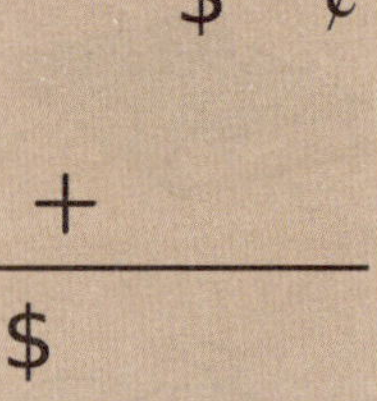

$ ¢

\+

$

50 cents + 50 cents = 100 cents or $1

$1 + $2 = $ ____________

+

= $ ________

+

= $ ________

—

= $ ________

Add

25 cents + 10 cents ________ ________	50 cents + 25 cents ________ ________	75 cents + 20 cents ________ ________

Subtract

45 cents − 15 cents ________ ________	90 cents − 40 cents ________ ________	80 cents − 20 cents ________ ________

REVIEW EXERCISE 4

Fill in the blanks

a. __________ comes before Wednesday.

b. __________ comes after March

c. A square has __________ sides

d. A __________ has no sides.

e. The short hand of the clock is called the __________ hand.

Draw the hands of the clock to show the time.

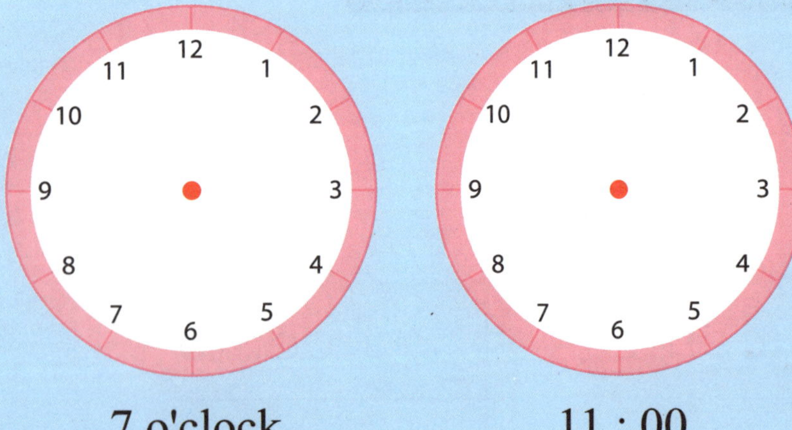

7 o'clock   11 : 00

Match the following

Break fast time	Two 1 cent coins
Lunch time	1:00 p.m.
First day of the week	Monday
Heavy	a sack of potatoes
A 10 dollar bill	Five 2 dollar bills
$ 2	9 : 00 a.m.